BETWEEN THE MOUNTAIN
AND THE SKY

BETWEEN

the

MOUNTAIN

and the

SKY

A MOTHER'S STORY OF LOVE,
LOSS, HEALING, AND HOPE

MAGGIE DOYNE

with SHANNON LEE MILLER

HARPER HORIZON

Published by Harper Horizon, an imprint of HarperCollins Focus LLC.

Any internet addresses, phone numbers, or company or product information printed in this book are offered as a resource and are not intended in any way to be or to imply an endorsement by Harper Horizon, nor does Harper Horizon vouch for the existence, content, or services of these sites, phone numbers, companies, or products beyond the life of this book.

ISBN 978-0-7852-4029-7 (eBook)
ISBN 978-0-7852-4028-0 (HC)
ISBN 978-0-7852-4043-3 (SC)

Library of Congress Control Number: 2021941639

Printed in the United States of America
23 24 25 26 27   LSC   10 9 8 7 6 5 4 3 2 1

Contents

CONTENTS

Dear Reader,

Thank you for taking time out of your story to live in mine. It might seem like a small act, but your support, curiosity, and love mean more than you know.

In the beginning at Kopila Valley, before reliable Wi-Fi and even electricity, books were my greatest comfort, my best friends, and my deepest connections to the rest of the world. If you find solace or hope in these pages, if you see even a glimpse of yourself or your family, I'll consider this first book of mine a roaring success.

For the past twelve years, I've been part of a team raising a group of amazing children at Kopila Valley Children's Home in Surkhet, Nepal. There are so many stories to tell about this beautiful place and its even more beautiful people, but my story is the only one that belongs to me, and the only one I'm qualified to tell. It is my biggest, brightest hope that, one day, our children and the rest of our team will choose to share their lives with you, but when they do, it will be on their own terms. You'll still get to know them enough through these pages to fall madly in love.

Another story I feel unqualified to tell is that of international development, a complex, ethically challenging, rapidly changing field of work I'm honored to have stumbled into. I am passionate about making this world better, and I'm happy to be able to share my experience, but it is merely *one* experience. This is not a how-to guide. I've made many mistakes, and I still have a lot to learn.

Between the Mountain and the Sky spans more than a decade, during which I moved to Nepal, built a house, raised fifty-four children, endured trauma, and experienced the wildest love imaginable. "Mom brain" is real, and my memory is imperfect. I relied heavily on blog entries, journals, and the (much more reliable) minds of those who have been at my side. Conversations have been reconstructed as best as I could remember them, with plenty of care taken to preserve veracity and meaning. Also, some names and identifying details have been changed to protect anyone who I thought may not want to make a cameo in a memoir.

Thank you, thank you, thank you for being here.

Big Love,
Maggie

Prologue
SUNRISE

EARLY IN THE day, when the sun is still shy behind the mountains, the children and I cross the street in front of our house and walk down the dirt path to our small bamboo school. We pass yellow mustard fields and tin-roofed houses dressed up with coral paint. Street dogs come to sniff our ankles, chickens squawk, and the neighbors wave at us. We're quite the group, a family of more than fifty all together, and on any given day, half of us are skipping, shuffling, or marching up the road through the morning mist. I'm the mother figure to fifty-four children, sister to half a dozen "aunties" and "uncles" who live and work and parent alongside me, wife to Jeremy, and "mama" to our biological daughter, Ruby. Surkhet, a foothill town in midwestern Nepal, is our home.

Our mornings are a precious frenzy, as they are for parents and caregivers all over the world. There are just more of us here. Shangkar Uncle and Basanti Auntie wake early and make a big, steaming pot of chai before starting on breakfast. The crushing of ginger and grinding of fresh black pepper and cardamom are the first sounds I hear, and the smell, milky and sweet and comforting, draws all the adults from our beds to the kitchen. Tope, my cofounder, and his wife, Kusum, will soon head off on their morning walk with our dogs, Nova and Nacho. Tope has his head-phones in and the news from BBC radio on. He takes them off and gives us a play-by-play of anything and everything that's happened in Nepal and the rest of the world overnight. Aakriti and Sachyam, our head caregivers, ring the breakfast bell.

Through the kitchen window, I watch Namraj skateboard by and Sukma Auntie comb Pabitra's hair into pigtails on the porch. Santosh joins her, complaining that he's lost his belt. Sundar has two right shoes, and Asmita's uniform is still wet from being left out in the rain overnight. A game of walnut marbles begins in the side yard, and kids swing on the swing set in the garden. The bell rings again, and they all come running, walnuts in hand, bickering about who won the game. Basanti appears carrying a big pot of *sujji* (sweet cream of wheat) and a basket of bananas.

"Counting!" Sachyam shouts.

The children arrive, falling in line and calling out their numbers, one to fifty-four. First there are the littlest ones, Khushbu, Himal, and Jamuna. Then the six-to-eight-year-olds, Jhagat, Pabitra, Asmita, and Manisha, a flash of green in their uniforms. The middle kids follow: Kalpana, Ganga, Hari, Khajuri, Man Kumari, Shanti, Yagay, Maya, Bindu, and Santosh. The teenagers come last: Krishna Bogati, Naveen, Padam, Hansaraj, Anjali, Sagar, Alina, Sanju, Bhakta, Rupa, and little Nisha. The teens refer to themselves as the "originals" and have been at Kopila Valley Children's Home since the beginning. They remember carrying the bricks upstairs to build the third story, bathing and washing our clothes in the spring at Bulebule. They remember when we got our first TV, dug the first well, and when Sudip and Nirmal got arrested for shoplifting.

The young adults are grown up now and scattered all over the world. Shova is at Lafayette College in Pennsylvania, and Janak is at Drew University in New Jersey, where I'm from. There's Nisha in Senegal, Goma at King's College, Keshav at Midwestern University, and Karma at nursing school. I miss them most in the mornings, but as they move on, their numbers are passed to new children, most recently Kiran and Sunita, who sit next to each other and eat three bananas each. When the meal is over, ready or not, we set off through the front gates.

Our elementary school across the street is nothing impressive, but it's the heartbeat of the community. We built it when I was twenty-two. It's just some bamboo, tin, and plyboard laid on slabs of stone and cement. Games of Ping-Pong and freeze tag begin at sunrise and also a Nepali game called "Fire in the Mountain" that kind of reminds me of "Duck, Duck, Goose." There's a small entryway and a large blue sign that reads KOPILA VALLEY SCHOOL. Grandmothers, big sisters, aunties, uncles, and neighbors gather to drop off their little ones and say, "Namaste." The kids freshly dressed from our home run past me toward their friends and teachers, and only a few of them bother to stop for a kiss goodbye. The big yellow Kopila bus rolls by, and dew begins to lift from the playground. The school bell rings. Everything falls quiet. I take a long walk through town.

The beauty and majesty of this landscape hasn't faded one bit since I first set eyes on it twelve years ago at age nineteen. The foggy green foothills and gentle, trickling river are ageless, but everything around them has changed. Over the last decade, Surkhet, traditionally little more than a stopover for people going from rural villages to the Indian border for migrant work, has made the shift from trading post to bustling town. The ready-made clothing shops, which only sold saris and kurtas when I arrived as a traveler on my gap year, now have denim pants and button-down shirts in the windows. There are more cars on the roads, and the roads are covered in thick, shimmering blacktop. I still remember the day the first ATM arrived in 2010. Hundreds of people gathered around to see "the money machine."

The things that make this place home, though, have stayed exactly as they were: the fruit and vegetable sellers sitting on the ground with their eggplants, bitter gourd, and kafal berries from the mountains; the yellow glare of the jewelry store; the local pharmacist who, after my years of parenting sick kids, knows me by name. The sound of butchers slaughtering chickens and goats hangs in the air, one life ending to nourish another.

Inevitably, even if it isn't on my way, I wander toward the riverbed. A new bridge stretches from one bank to the other now, so you don't have to wade through muck during monsoon. Mud and straw huts sit on the edge of the banks, turrets of smoke pouring from their open roofs. I listen for the dissonant ring of mallet against stone shuddering through the air like broken church bells, but it's not there. Through the years, I've gotten to know the families here. They are laborers, porters, migrants, domestic servants, and farmworkers.

"Good morning, Maggie Miss!"

I wave back to a young mother from the new bridge, and I notice the baby on her back. She has bright eyes like Ruby's and cheeks as impossibly chubby as Khushi's. The mother sways with the baby on her back, a motion my own hips will never forget. People rush across the little overpass behind me on bicycles and in tiny cars, eyes up, staring south into the endless stretch of rice paddies or north into the mountains. Surrounded by the Himalayan foothills, under feathery clouds and hot white sun, the most beautiful thing I see is a mother loving a child.

1

ROCK-BREAKING GIRL

Dear B,
You almost go unnoticed, but I see you.
—M

THE RIVER IN Surkhet is on Nepali time. It wanders slowly down from the mountains in the Karnali Zone of midwestern Nepal, arriving quiet and exhausted, at barely a trickle, in the center of town. Crawling past the pushcarts and vegetable stands, the cobbler and the transient sacred cows, the water dries up completely, leaving nothing but its luggage of silt and trash in a bone-gray cradle. Rivers are considered holy in this part of the world. You bathe in them and worship in them, whether they rush clear through the foothills or squirm through the mud. Many of the people I've met here say that the river is where you go when you die. But the river is where Hima lives.

The first time I see her, she's a streak of orange, a curl of tangerine skin sitting in the dirt. Rising from the belly of the riverbed, she dusts off the bright, puffy sleeves of what in a previous life must've been a party dress, and gets to work.

She can't be older than five, I guess, standing at the lip of the bank.

I watch her weave between slabs of plastic and cinder blocks and scoop up a stone the size of a soccer ball, waddling it back to her pile of gravel and grunting like a quarryman. She sits cross-legged and whacks the rock over and over, brows scrunched so close that they meet.

No matter where I go, I always seem to end up in places like this one—alleyways, outskirts, trash heaps—the back pockets of a place where less desirable things and people get stuffed away. I've been traveling all over the South Pacific and living in India on my gap year, but still, a mix of sadness, fear, and shame hits me under my tongue every time I see these hidden, tucked-away places. Little kids go to work in some places. They're porters, laborers on construction sites, domestics, agricultural workers. Watching them work is jarring—watching them work with a smile, even more so. The girl pulls herself up, shakes the pebble from her skirt, and sizes up a new hunk of shale.

Beyond the territory she's staked out in the gully, there are others, all women and children as far as I can see—a coalition of them. Some look thin. Some smile through their sweat and red tikka and patterned, beautifully colored *deutis*. Nearly all of them look tired, worn ragged and caked in a layer of dust from the riverbed. They wander up and down, looking for rock material they can crush into gravel and sell to developers and road construction projects. After roughly a decade of civil war in Nepal, money is coming in again, and people are building homes, especially in this tiny trading post of a town. In 2006, unsuspecting Surkhet, with its rickety mango stands and freewheeling livestock, is beginning to grow. Plots that were once rice paddies are sold off by the *katta*—lots of about 3,600 square feet—and transformed into boxy mud, tin, and brick homes.

Although Surkhet was never fully infiltrated by the Maoists or the government forces, there are quiet, almost polite remains of conflict. Checkpoints with armed guards surround the valley. Soldiers do their morning patrols through the streets, jogging with long, symmetrical strides. Despite these reminders of conflict, it's borderline idyllic, a paradise in one of the poorest regions in one of the poorest countries in the world. In the town center, children hang on the statue of beloved King Birendra like he's Mickey Mouse (though I think he looks more like Jack Nicholson), and a bakery that could have been plucked straight from *Beauty and the Beast* shows off perfectly crescent-shaped samosas and *pao roti* from behind a window. There are more baked goods than bullet holes. The remains of hammer-and-sickle graffiti are worn and almost washed away from monsoon rains. The Himalayan districts just north of here are still in tatters.

Crossing the river is the quickest way back to my hostel, so I start to shimmy down, clods of dry, sun-bleached earth buckling under my feet and turning suddenly into mud in the basin. The peppery smell of chai that followed me here from the tea shop refuses to go any further. Cardamom and clove dig their heels in. The scents of human waste and sweaty goat take over. Breathing through my mouth, I ignore the ominous squishing sound that comes up from the bottom of my trekker boots, the wetness that tickles my toes. I try to go unnoticed, feeling a little ashamed, as always, to be happy and fed. Meanwhile life in the river rushes on, starving.

A baby strapped to the back of an older child begins to wail. In Nepal, the girl, about fourteen, could be either his sister or his mother. Another baby starts, pitching his apricot-sized fist into the air. Then another. A tiny infant union forms instantly and decides to go on strike. Caregivers start off toward the block of shanty homes made of old rice bags and corrugated metal.

My friend in the orange dress looks up from her hammering. Her eyes, flecked with gold and lack of sleep, lock onto mine. After traveling and traveling and traveling, I can't go another step.

What am I supposed to do? In this moment, in this life? What are we, as a human family, supposed to do and be?

She drops her mallet, and I look at her as if she has the answers. She looks at me like she *is* the answer.

"Namaste, *didi*," she shouts, frantically waving her leathery doll hand my way. A giant sun-soaked smile practically explodes between her cheeks.

Hello, big sister. My Nepali isn't great, but I know this phrase. Everyone is everyone's *didi* here.

I take a long look at her. She takes a long look at me.

"Namaste," I say back.

The population of the universe dwindles to exactly two: a teenager from Jersey who spent her childhood bouncing on an enormous backyard trampoline and trying to get good grades, and a dalit, an "untouchable" who has never seen a school or a toilet. Sifting shoeless through the trash and grinning like a goofy cartoon, there she is, the world's most unspeakable failure and its unending promise, all tied up with a thin orange ribbon. The plates inside me begin to shift.

I keep walking, knowing with certainty that I'll see her again, crossing the river and letting her perfect bird voice echo in my head. *Namaste, didi.*

In another life, she could be my sister.

In another life, she could be me.

I HAVEN'T ALWAYS known to ask the big questions about humanity, or try to understand why some people had so much and some people had hardly anything, why most of the people I met that did have so much seemed exclusively white and beautiful. When you grow up like that, you don't know to question it. I have always loved my home, a blue split-level in New Jersey, with two sisters, progressive, earthy parents, and a trampoline bigger than the mud huts where people sleep in Nepal. I was grateful for everything I had but you can also only compare to what's around you.

The questions got bigger as I did, and though school was a joyful distraction, with algebra and boys and soccer, it never gave me answers I needed. In 2005, I sat down at the breakfast table and told my parents I wasn't going to college right away. There were things I needed to figure out. I was going on a gap year. I would be a useful human while trying to understand what being a good human meant. They're free-spirited adventurers at heart, so they didn't seem to mind at all.

My first semester was with a group of other seventeen-to-twenty-year-olds focusing on travel, cultural immersion, experiential learning, and life skills outside the four walls of a classroom. While it was still a group of privileged young adults who looked mostly like me, it did give me a taste of the world outside what I'd been exposed to. We spent a month under palm leaves as big as canoes, building a seawall in the South Pacific. Then there was the silent retreat at the Buddhist monastery, learning the power of meditation with nuns and monks. They asked us during our orientation to leave the toilet lids down so bugs wouldn't fall in and die. We moved onto a farm and learned how to WWOOF (organic farm), which in my case was just scooping chicken poop and getting sent out on the hundreds of acres of farm to cut manuka, an invasive and devilish plant. We took an outdoor survival course in New Zealand. In Australia, we explored the outback and got eaten alive by bush flies. I got my belly button pierced and learned to surf.

My friend Hannah, who I'd met during the first semester, convinced me that we just "had to" go to India together for our last and final few months before starting college and resuming the lives that our small upper-middle-class towns had plotted out for us. Because we just "had to," we did. We worked at a school and children's home and center on the banks of the Ganges.

There were a lot of children at Ramana's Garden—refugee kids from Nepal, young girls and boys who had been trafficked, abused, and discarded, children of the war. It was different there than the monastery, the farm, or the outback. I was learning so much every day being there taken in by the kids, the tiles in the house, the banyan tree. Life inside the gates of Ramana's was filled with laughter; there was song and cheerfulness, defying every sorrow from which it was born. I spent my days playing marbles in the courtyard with the boys and showing the girls their faces over and over in the Canon PowerShot my parents got me for graduation. With every giggle and silly face and pair of pee-soaked pants, the answers to the big questions inched closer.

Am I supposed to be a teacher?

Am I supposed to head back to New Jersey and go to college?

We were supposed to stay for a few months. But Hannah returned to the United States to start college at Cornell and I decided to stay on for another year. I felt like I had more to learn. Prabha, the director of Ramana's, saw something in me. She took me under her wing and taught me everything she knew. She gave me one responsibility after another. I learned the most from the people working there. There was a kind man named Tope who managed the day-to-day logistics of life around the compound and the various outreach programs. He was always helpful, seemed to know the answers to everyone's questions and problems, and worked hard, while whistling and smiling and blaring Nepali music in his old blue jeep he called the gypsy. Tope and his wife, Kusum, were Nepali refugees themselves. They cared for the children, cooked meals, drove them to the doctor for checkups, and tucked their little bodies into bed, as though it were the most important, most revered work in the world.

The longer I stayed there, the surer I was that they were right.

———

I MET SUNITA at Ramana's. Unlike me, Sunita knew exactly where she was going in life—to medical school to become a doctor. Her big question in life was where she came from. It had been eight years since Sunita had returned to her country and her village, and as her memories started to fade, she had questions. She's Tope's niece. We became fast friends and we made a plan to go to Nepal and find her village.

Weeks later, she and I are staying at the Namaste Nepal, the glitziest, most touristy hostel we could find in Surkhet. It's no Four Seasons, but it has hot water, bed linens, and a restaurant that serves cloud-shaped dumplings called *momos*, filled with a meat Sunita convinces me is goat.

"Maggie!" she practically screams my name. I plow through the door and almost knock her over. She mutters a string of what I imagine are filthy Nepali swear words.

"I met someone!" I scream back.

Sunita is sixteen, only two years younger than me, but she's tougher and wiser. Being forced to leave your village and your family at the age of six makes you grow up fast. Before we got to Surkhet, we'd spent weeks trekking through the Himalayas to Oda, the village she fled when she was eight to escape the war. She went to live with Tope and Kusum in India so that she could go to school, the ultimate luxury for a rural Nepali girl. When I met her, she told me that the memories of the village she came from were beginning to fade. I promised her, a bit heroically, I thought, that as soon as the government reached an armistice with the Maoists and everything was safe, I would go there with her. A few months later, Sunita was on a school break and we started to plan our trip to her village. When I agreed to this trip to Nepal together, I had no idea what I was in for.

We trekked for days, *up, up, up*, into the Himalayas, across the thigh-melting summit of Maha Bua, and down, almost stumbling onto her village, Oda. It appeared behind a thick, glassy plate of sunshine, when I swore I couldn't take another step, spilling out of the mountainside like a grand, green staircase of terraced buckwheat plots, shaggy grass-roofed huts, and mountain sheep. So, so many sheep.

We stayed weeks, harvesting the fields, fetching water from the spring, and padding the sides of the buildings with clay and buffalo dung. Sunita's closest family was mostly gone, and her family's hut had been ruined, converted into some kind of Maoist clubhouse and later destroyed, which didn't seem to bother her. Oda was still home, and these people were still family, some related by blood and others by simply being. It made sense. Everything made sense. One woman cared for the cows, another milked them. Someone made corn or buckwheat chappati, balls of dough flattened with a wooden roller and then held over the fire. We all ate them together, with the rice and corn stored up from the dry season. The intrinsic ties between all of us were as visible and immovable as the mountains behind us.

When it was time to leave, our bodies were lean, and our skin had grown dark and scuffed like animal hide. The village aunties cried and made us promise to come back. Sunita had found many of the answers she was looking for. Now I had to.

Today, in a dry river in a stopover town, I'd found a little girl who reminded me of myself.

Sunita clears her throat. "Maggie?"

She's getting impatient *and* running late to meet relatives.

"Sunita, I met a girl in the river. Maybe we can help her. I feel like I have to."

———————

I'M NOT THE first white girl to cross an ocean with a backpack to try to find herself on (well, near) a mountain. I read *Eat, Pray, Love*, and I read it hard. I didn't leave home to save the world. I just left to see it, to *know* it—maybe to know and see myself. But maybe seeing yourself is how these things begin.

Over the past year, I've seen and probably participated in a lot of mistakes: bushy-tailed, Bible-bustin' missionaries eager to build churches but not schools, environmentalists who want to save the local "whatchamathing" while it decimates local food crops. Those kinds of things. I have been the overeager white kid building the wall that the locals could have built. Colonialism with a good heart is still colonialism.

I want to help the girl get out of the river, but only if that's what she wants and if that's what help really is. It's not my place to say what she or anybody else here needs.

First, I decide to ask Google what she needs. I set up shop at Surkhet's finest and only internet café and spend all day banging my head against a wall of bootleg DVDs. I search "life in postwar Nepal" and am immediately overwhelmed.

One in twenty children is an orphan.

Only half of the women in the country over age six have ever attended school.

Nearly 60 percent of the population in the Karnali midwestern region are living in poverty.

The answer to the question that seemed baffling—how a little girl ends up crushing stone in a slum—now seems perfectly, heart-breakingly clear. But how to help, how to even begin to help, is still murky.

A slow-moving fan in the corner of the shop wheezes in the heat, and I look around. Aside from the clerk, I'm the only person here. My Coca-Cola spits and crackles. Bright swaths of sari fabric graze the edges of the open door, and occasionally, I hear a breath or two of music. I'm asking the internet questions about the Surkhet when it's right there waiting for me. I pack up my things, pay my bill, and begin asking questions to the locals I've met.

I meet up with Sunita. I ask her six thousand questions about her life, which could have gone so differently if she hadn't left Nepal during the war for an education all those years ago. Then, we meet Mimkosha, a brilliant, enterprising woman who owns a textile shop in the center of town. She's self-made, a true success story, but she doesn't know how to write her own name. We talk with community leaders and elders, women crushing stone and selling cucumbers. I call Tope, whom we haven't talked to since we arrived late in Surkhet, and he's furious. He was convinced we'd been pulverized by two stories' worth of snow in Kalikot or sold as Communist brides.

"Maggie," he says, "education isn't free here. Many families can't afford it. Children need to work so that their families can eat."

I listen and take everything in. Poor little girls work. Then they get married. Then they work again, brand-new babies buckled tight to their backs instead of books. School is an extravagance; it costs money. For many families, sending a working child to class every day could mean a significant loss of household income. It could mean more poverty, less nutrition, and no way to survive. Then there's tuition.

"Remember, Maggie," Tope says before we hang up, "you can't help everyone."

A few days into my fact-finding mission, I invite a school principal that Mimkosha knows for lemon tea. *Tuition* is a scary word in America, but I want to find out exactly what it would take to enroll the little girl in school.

"Twelve hundred rupees, Maggie, *bahini* [little sister]," he offers politely.

Her tuition would be ten American dollars. Replacing her income would be less than a dollar per day. I try not to let my jaw drop into my teacup.

SUNITA COMES WITH me to the riverbed the next day, a punishing one-hundred-degree afternoon where everything, not just the river, moves on Nepali time. I point to an orange skirt whooshing around like a comet tail, and the little girl recognizes me right away.

"Namaste, didi," she warbles, bringing her hands to her chest in prayer.

Sunita squats down, smiles, and asks her name. I thank God I have a translator.

"Hima," she declares proudly, sorting through a bundle of trash and picking up an aluminum can caked in green sludge.

We find out where she's from (Surkhet), how old she is (seven, not five as I'd guessed), and if she has any family (no father, but a mother who works in the river too). Then Sunita asks her if she'd like to go to school.

Hima stops.

Her eyes open wide, and she lets out a series of ridiculous squeals. Fast and frenzied words that even Sunita can't catch pour out of her as she hops around us, ricocheting off one bank of the river and then the next.

Sunita laughs. "Hima says she'd like to go to school more than anything in the world."

Before we can think of what to do next, Hima grabs our hands and drags us with shocking force toward her mom. Hima's mom looks strong, almost Amazonian, with fabric wrapped around her lower back for support as she extracts rubble from the bank. She turns out to be even more excited than her daughter.

Two weeks later, dressed in a burgundy checked shirt, blue slacks, and a necktie half the length of her body, with the cuckoos announcing her and an audience of black snuffling pigs, Hima walks out of the riverbed and onward. I head back to the hotel.

It's almost time for Sunita and me to leave Surkhet. In a few days, we'll be in Pokhara, fawning over the incredibly blue lakes. A few days after that, we'll hit Kathmandu, or the "Du." Sunita swears only I have ever called it that. Eventually, from there, I'll make my way back home to college applications. That was always the plan: wander off the path for a year and then hop back on.

I mourn every breath of chai smell that sneaks into my nose on the walk back to Namaste Nepal. Dry season is dwindling; the air is thick and heavy. Soon the ground will turn green, the riverbed will fill, and the squatters will scatter, going God knows where to do God knows what. Mimkosha and Sunita are chatting about one of the big festivals, Dashain or Tihar, but I can hardly hear them. All I can hear is the sounds of the river, and hammer on stone.

As we make plans to leave I wonder, as a human family, how in the world have we let a river fill with more child laborers than water? Hima is in school and has a chance. But what about the others? For the price of a pair of jeans, lives could change forever. Nepal could change forever.

"Namaste," a lady selling smiles at me.

"Namaste, didi." I bow back at her.

Nepali music spills from the shops—the internet café and the place with the pots and pans, and the bank, which is about the size of my parents' closet. I pick out the hollow pop of a *dholak* drum from the music and a *sarangi*, which looks like a fat violin and always sounds a bit worried to me. I begin to hum along.

We reach the end of the main drag, and the music gets lost between the slow-talking cows and the gurgle of an old bus. The deep chime of the rock breakers takes over again, ringing out toward Oda, far off in the green of the mountains. I remember how simple and how good a life *together* can be.

Over the next few days, we enroll five more children in school.

2

BRICK BY BRICK

Dear N,
When I think of you, I think of blocks, blocks, and more
blocks. You love to build things with your hands and have
been good with a shovel and dirt since you were two.

—M

HIMA BURIES HER head into my belly and says goodbye, wrapping her arms around my waist and squeezing tight like a hungry boa.

"*Pheri bhetaula*," I tell her and her mother, handling each syllable slowly and with care, desperate not to mispronounce the goodbye I say to them.

Sunita and I are leaving for the lake district today, bracing ourselves for seventeen hours on a Nepali bus, a passenger experience that can only be understood if you've spent significant time on a mechanical bull.

"Are you okay?" Sunita asks as we slowly tear ourselves away from the riverbed.

"I think so. But I might cry or throw up on the bus." I smile.

She laughs. Somebody is always throwing up on those buses.

We promise Tope, who is still convinced we're moments away from getting kidnapped or eaten by snow leopards, that we'll call him before we set off. Sunita stops by a roadside phone near the King Birendra statue, and I pace around.

I listen to them chatter and try my best to soak up every single particle of Surkhet that floats my way: the smell of far-off mountain air, diesel, and chai. The songs the kids sing that I can't understand but love just the same. Laundry and prayer flags strung up from anything that agrees to hold them. King Birendra—giant, concrete, freckled with bird poop, but still charming.

For a tired, delusional second, I swear he winks at me.

Goodbye, big guy, I think, and I drag myself over to Sunita, who is nodding wildly at the receiver.

"Sure!" she exclaims. "We'd love to go check on your property, Tope Uncle. Maggie can take pictures!"

She points at the Canon, which is looking as weary as I am. We set out on one last Surkhet adventure, stopping by the fabric shop to recruit Mimkosha.

WE FOLLOW A skinny road out past the riverbed and walk straight into the horizon for what feels like an entire afternoon. White, hot, and high in the sky, the sun reminds the mountains that they aren't as big as they think they are, and it pours down onto us, making the walk feel more like a trek than it should.

During the war, Tope wanted to buy land for his sister as an investment. The economy was a mess, and land felt like a safe place to invest money. He wanted something in Oda, near home, but when he arrived from India to look, the Maoists were all over the mountain. Tope—who, even on a good day, is not a thrill seeker—decided on Surkhet instead. He found a few meters of flat parcel outside town and hasn't seen it for a year.

After about half an hour, we hear children's voices and the rubbery thud of feet passing a soccer ball. Simple homes begin to spring up around us into a kind of suburb. Echoes of my own childhood carry me back in time and plunk me right down on Collins Avenue, with Libby and Kate, my sisters, comparing cartwheels and bickering in the yard. We had absolutely everything back then and absolutely no concept of just how much everything was. I'm only beginning to wrap my brain around privilege. I wasn't even aware of it until I arrived at Ramana's Garden. Until I met Hima and the other kids. Until I realized that while I was busy eating frozen yogurt with my siblings, Sunita was milking a cow in Oda and helping to raise her siblings.

I scan the neighborhood for the budding soccer stars, but they're distant specks.

An older man with a belly is standing next to an unremarkable patch of dirt, loudly discharging the phlegm from his throat.

"That's it!" Sunita says, waving to the landlord.

The land is parched and cracked, covered in a web of empty veins. Shangri-La it isn't. Wordlessly, it cries out for something: rain, grass, shade, a shovel, a goat or two . . . anything to drag it out of complete desolation. I cross from the road over a feathery patch of grass barely clinging to the earth and onto Tope's property, expecting it to moan when I sink my weight down.

I take my camera out and begin snapping pictures, willing the Canon to be kind to the place. The plot isn't very big, a handful of meters wide and a few more long. Its prized and only possession is a single stunted tree that reaches skyward as proudly as it can. I try not to gawk at it and wonder how anything could grow here, rooted in what feels like solid rock.

"It's a very good investment, you know," Mimkosha pipes up. She can tell I'm not impressed. I've never been good at hiding my bewilderment, and it's probably worse when I try.

"Really?" I ask.

Mimkosha nods excitedly, which thankfully brings a bit of color to the place.

"Since Tope put the first deposit on the land just one year ago, the price has already tripled, and with the way things are going in town, the value will only go up." She nods approvingly at Tope's purchase as she talks. "So much is growing here, Maggie."

I look at the tree one more time. Silently, it agrees with her.

I can still hear the kids in the street behind us. A shrieking, squeaking pack of girls have joined in, and they're all playing a new game now. I can't guess what it is. My chest seizes up a bit, and I think of the river, of the children who know how to crush a rock into the perfect pebble but don't know how to play tag, who haul bags of rice on their backs and live without clean water. Hima, in the universe of that river, is lucky. She goes to school. She has a mother. We met so many children who had nothing.

Just like Tope, I think.

Suddenly, my blood begins to pump faster, and my mind stops wandering. It lands at Ramana's Garden.

"How much did Tope pay for the land?" I ask Mimkosha. She spins around and her beautiful cat eyes grow wide with surprise.

"Well," she calculates, "he bought this for about two hundred dollars per square meter, and now the going rate is about eight hundred dollars . . ."

"Are they selling more?" I ask, snipping off her string of equations. She grins, watching the gears in my head groan into action.

Sunita curiously peeks over at us from her conversation with the landlord.

"I'm not going to ask in front of him," Mimkosha whispers. "I don't want him to think we're interested, *but* I'm pretty sure this entire lot next to Tope's is for sale."

The sun softens above us, excusing itself for a moment to duck behind a cloud. I walk over to the poor tree and give it a pat, like it's an old, white-nosed dog. My hand rests on the soft, almost fluffy bark, and I lean my weight into it for a minute, shocked by how easily it holds me, how strongly it's rooted here. Looking through the brittle branches, the empty land now looks full to me. I see a swing set and a small soccer pitch, a bright yellow house with arches and terra-cotta tiles, a vegetable garden with green paddles of lettuce and ugly-beautiful tomatoes barely clinging onto the vine. I see a home.

I turn to Mimkosha. "I'll talk to Tope, but I think I want to buy it."

We're going to build a home, and a community center, for Nepali children, right here. There isn't a shred of doubt in my mind.

I'M SURE EVERY parent wants to raise a kid who wants to move to a remote corner of the world and work with children. I'm not so sure that every parent wants to raise a kid who actually does it. I wait three and a half days to call my parents.

"Hello? *Hello?!* Can you hear me, Dad?"

The connection is terrible. Crackling and buzzing and stuttering. It seems more nervous than I am.

"Maggie? Is that you? I can barely hear you. . . . Are you still in Nepal?"

"Yeah, Dad, I'm in Surkhet. Listen, I have something important . . ."

I'm glad that my dad picks up first. He's a gentle guy, long-haired
and a little kooky. During my formative years, he worked at a health
food store and stayed home with us, making sure we logged more
hours outside than in. He meditated and went to sweat lodges and
kept a small Buddha on our mantle, which he never explained to us
but which we loved anyway. My dad stuck out like a sore thumb in
buttoned-up, preppy Mendham, New Jersey.

If anybody's going to leap on board with me, it's probably
going to be him.

Before I can clear my throat, he stops me.

"Hold on, Maggie—let me get your mom."

"Wait, Dad . . . !"

It's too late. I hear her fumbling around with the receiver.

Mom is tougher, a realtor. A good realtor who could sell snow
to Santa Claus. Growing up, her adoration was impossible to
ignore, but it showed up more as tenacity than tenderness. Her
life's goal was to give us every opportunity in the world and raise
three strong young women. She worked hard for us. She had to.

"Maggie, is something wrong?" she frets.

Mercifully, they spend a few minutes bickering about whose
background noise is noisier, not knowing they're about to be
stunned. Of three daughters, I'm the least likely to move to Nepal.
I'm the predictable one, the anxious kid, afraid of earthquakes
(Nepal has those) and avalanches (those too) and snakes (buckets
of those). I was scooped up in tears from every sleepover I ever
attended. More than anything, what I wanted was to be home
with my parents. They were good parents. They didn't lionize a

particular god or politician (though they did demonize a few). In their own ways they'd carved their own paths off the beaten track of "normal" suburban parenting. They didn't pretend to fit the mold. Often, I longed for them to pretend a little harder. Whether I ran into it with arms wide open or not, I grew up with freedom of heart, mind, and spirit. It was more than a happy childhood—it was a childhood filled with love.

"So, here's the thing." I clear my throat. "I need you to get five thousand dollars out of my savings account and send it to me as soon as possible."

It's quiet. Even the background noises stop.

My mom speaks first. "But you've been saving that money since you were a kid! That's your college money!"

Before I can throw "Surprise! I'm not going to college!" back at her, my dad talks.

"What on earth do you need all that money for?"

"I'm going to buy a piece of property in Surkhet and build a home for children."

Some background noises resume: footsteps, tapping, big, big sighs. I can practically see my mom's face through the phone, crumpled up and wondering if this is what becomes of a liberal child with unfettered access to the wilderness and animal totems and granola. And my dad, my poor dad, asking himself if this is what he gets for driving us up to school in the junky blue van and having the gall to honk in front of the football players. I always promised I'd get him back for it.

"I love you," I offer. I don't know what else to say, and it's honestly all I've got.

"We love you too."

A few days later, the money comes through, and the land purchase is complete. The words I lost on the phone finally reappear to me. It's simple and unrefined, but it's true.

I want to give these kids what you gave to me: a childhood filled with love and opportunity to be a child without having to worry about your most basic human needs like how many rocks you'll break in a day or when the next meal will come.

SIX MONTHS MELT together into soup. Sunita goes back to school in India. I miss her terribly, but she's well on her way to a full scholarship, and we joke that, one day, I'll need a doctor to revive me after I die in a sea of NGO (non-governmental organization) paperwork that I can't read.

I go home for a while, too, back to Jersey, but I'm so busy I feel like I'm suspended over an ocean the entire time, dangling somewhere between Mendham and Surkhet. My days consist of babysitting for whoever will hire me and frantically emailing Tope, who wholeheartedly agrees to partner with me. I read every single book I can get my hands on: *The White Man's Burden* by William Easterly; *Development as Freedom* by Amartya Sen; papers and studies published by a random cornucopia of NGOs and development experts. There is no "how-to" guide, and I know I'm entering into morally ambiguous territory. I use each book, each study, as a mirror, and I don't always like what I see. There are layers and consequences of development work I hadn't thought about.

There are rewards I've inherited because of who I am, where I was raised, and what I look like. Once I started, I couldn't stop examining them. I've been an unwitting participant in exploitation, racism, and sexism pretty much my entire life. All the time

I spent achieving in this world was also time I spent complicit in the systems that betray it. The more I research, the more I see that the futures of these kids will depend as much on my ability to deconstruct as they will on my ability to build.

Not much news about the Himalayas reaches us in suburban New Jersey, spitting distance from the Mendham Racquetball Club and the quaint local coffee shop, but my parents still keep a close, worried eye on Nepal the best that they can. We stand around the family computer and watch amateur protest footage from Kathmandu, men screaming, shattered store windows, fires grabbing at the air with their giant orange fingers. Even though the war is over, it doesn't quite seem like peace has begun either. I can't imagine what it takes for them to drive me to the airport, hug me, say, "I love you, be safe," and let go of everything they thought I would be.

————

WHEN I LAND in Surkhet, the weather is perfect, a windless seventy-five degrees, and the foothills are dressed in powdery red rhododendron tufts. Tope, his wife, Kusum, and Sunita's parents, Daju and Bauju, meet me at the airport. When you ask people in Nepal to help you, they actually show up in person.

"Welcome home." Tope smiles, watching me, watching the mountains, grabbing my poor backpack. "Beautiful, isn't it?"

It really, really is.

From there, we drive out to the house I rented and get to work. For months, work is all that we do.

May swallows the last bits of April, and the weather gets hot, so hot. Skin blisters, air trembles, and work crawls, but only when it has the energy. The days drip by like cold honey. Things are done slowly in Nepal; seeds are sown by hand, tea steeps and steeps and steeps. Obtaining permits and paperwork seems to be slowest of all. Nobody is in a hurry—least of all, it seems, the people whom we need to be.

The leftovers of the war provide a generous collection of interruptions to navigate. Buses full of Maoist outliers show up in town, and a curfew is imposed. Transportation workers strike, and the buses stop altogether. The young, wiry men with taut necks and raised fists, who should be on the buses, are burning tires in the streets of midwestern cities instead.

Finally, after a long string of days filled with meetings in Surkhet, the chief district officer is ready to stamp our registration, certifying a dream of a community-based organization working to empower children into reality. All we have left to do is come up with a name for the dream we've worked so hard to build.

We skitter out of the government building in the evening, like a bunch of sugar-drunk ants on a slice of watermelon, all of us—Tope, Kusum, Daju, Bauju, Mimkosha, and me—giddy for the first time in ages.

"We're almost there," I declare to no one in particular.

The men's shirts stick to their backs, and our shimmering, knee-length kurta tops make us feel, and probably look, like baked potatoes as we walk down the hill toward town. The sun is setting, and the temperature will drop soon. We stop and wait for it. Relief on every front feels reachable.

Peeling the fabric from our skin and looking down at Surkhet, we collectively smile at the shops and small network of roads that seem to bustle and bloom a little more each day, the bright painted homes, the promise of it all. There's a beautiful banyan tree that all of us seem to notice at the same time, right near the riverbed where I met Hima (who is totally crushing it in kindergarten).

The tree is stunning, an enormous, mighty tangle of roots. The long branches, all braided together, stretch impossibly far and wide, and they bear the glossiest and greenest leaves.

"What about 'root'? Something 'root'?" I ask, waiting for a Nepali translation.

"*Mūla*," Tope translates, then thinks on it for a minute. "Nah."

We keep spitballing, trying to capture the foothills, the rice paddies, which are just being planted, and the spirit of childhood in a single word. Maybe two. I throw out one botanical term after the next, but everything I suggest sounds like a dude ranch or an Indian buffet.

"Something happy, with color," Daju says, staring into the sun, sticking his hand to his head like a visor.

Bauju agrees. "And for the children," she adds, her nose ring jangling as she nods.

"What about Kopila?" Tope suggests, trying to temper the corners of a smile that have just started to show up on his face. "It's a bud just before it becomes a flower, and this will be a place where children bloom."

"Kopila *Valley*?" I ask, still looking out over the valley below us.

We all take turns saying it, then almost screaming it. The banyan tree shakes her leaves in agreement.

Kopila Valley. The perfect name. If a little bud has everything it needs to grow, it will flourish. With enough love, support, nutrition, and education, our kids will bloom too.

ON MY LAST night in Nepal, we break ground. Tope, Daju, a local legal advisor, and I finish writing the Kopila Valley bylaws, and we put together our local board, a body made up of just about everyone in Surkhet whom we know. Between the three of us, there isn't much money left, but we rent the house right next to our new Kopila Valley land, where Daju and Bauju will live with their children to oversee the construction, making their permanent return to Nepal after years waiting out the war in India. Tope and Kusum will go back to Ramana's Garden and work from there. I'll go back to America to make money, fill out even more paperwork, and hopefully find a way to keep us out of the red. I'm not sure what the process will look like. I've never even rented an apartment before, but we'll build this house brick by brick if we have to.

When the last colors of daytime begin to fall from the sky, it's time to measure out the foundation. We look over our construction plans. The land is small, and the house will need to be, too, only eight meters across, with room for a rain overhang. Even then, we'll graze the neighbor's land. It's tempting to use every inch of earth we have, but none of us have the heart to uproot that one lonely but persistent tree. It feels like a bit of a monument. Neighbors arrive with their tools to help us, and together, our shovels slice into the earth, carving out space for cement and iron, the backbone of Kopila Valley.

A local priest shows up in piles of thick orange robe just before the pitch-dark sets in. He's come to do a traditional land *pooja*, a ceremonial blessing that asks for Mother Earth's protection. Considering that we're about to give her a face-lift, it's the least we can do. There are a lot of rituals here, and so far, I love them. Festivals are wild and colorful. Even the simple act of arriving or saying goodbye seems to be an occasion for flowers around your neck and a red tikka on your forehead for luck. This pooja on such a perfect black-and-blue evening feels especially sacred.

The air becomes rich and smoky as the priest chants and wanders the lot, waving sticks of incense, pulsing orange at the ends.

Tendrils of sandalwood curl away from the glow and hang above us before getting lost in the sky. Our neighbors watch on beside us, shoulder to shoulder, heads bowed as the dark gets darker, a simple act of community that I would bottle if I could. I silently promise them that we'll do a good job; we'll cultivate and cherish the land; we'll raise good children and become gracious neighbors. I know as I stand here, with my Gap jeans and my atrocious Nepali, that welcoming me to their home is an act of faith.

Fat yellow marigold poms and spices arrive on a brass tray and are presented one by one, laid out by the priest in a careful formation on the cool, damp bottom of the cavity in the earth. The turmeric and bloody red *kumkum* powder are so bright I worry that the flowers might be jealous. The priest issues a grave, weighty prayer, and I let it root me, as I climb four feet down into the hole, as is the tradition, that will one day be the northeast corner of our home. Well, first I fall into the hole, but I right myself quickly. (Don't worry—everybody sees it happen.)

Sunk down into the earth, planted where the dirt is slick and the worms wiggle way up above, I stare upward and look for the light, taking incense and clay into my nose, my pores, the thickness of my hair. Dropping to my knees, I place a marigold into the center of the crater, hoping that I can bloom here too.

3

IN THE BLINK OF AN EYE

Dear Big B,
You have the most beautiful, enduring, resilient spirit. You
are also the most stubborn human being I've ever met in
my life.

—M

NEW JERSEY IS hot and cranky when I arrive in July 2007, bursting through the sliding doors in "Arrivals" with fire in my eyes and lice on my head. I cut through the grumbling shuffle of international travelers like an axe in a warm pat of butter. I'm barely 110 pounds, but I'm more of a person than I was when I left, and somehow I seem to take up more space. Months of *dhal bhat*, slow-simmered lentils and rice, along with hard work, have melted the fat from my hips and sculpted muscles where there were none. My skin is taut across my cheeks, and my hands are rough. I'm older now, almost twenty, but I know that with the silvery bags under my eyes and the crevices dug at their edges, I look a few years beyond where I am.

I see my dad leaning against the luggage carts, peering over the tops of heads to find me. At five foot four, I'm tall and leggy in Nepal, but here a bit of a pipsqueak. I peek out from under my backpack and wave. He jolts into a welcome.

"You're home!" He smiles.

Even though I smell like days of sweat and airplane food, he hugs me. His shoulders fall by inches in what I assume is relief, and I hang there in his arms. It's been such a long time since anything or anyone felt familiar. It takes me a second to remember that I'm a daughter.

He grabs my backpack, threadbare and no longer the vibrant blue it once was, and we start off toward the car.

"It's good to be home," I say. But I'm not sure where home is anymore.

It's almost the Fourth of July, and nobody in Mendham is keeping it a secret. Crisp, brand-new flags jerk in the wind instead of billow, and the neat little porches are all done up with tricolor buntings, fresh coats of paint, and planters full of petunias. It's radically quaint here, just as I left it. The ponds are still filled with koi fish the size of beef tenderloins, and the Mendham Creamery is still churning out perfectly spherical scoops. Even the birds agree to sing and not squawk.

There is nobody selling bitter gourd on the corner, there are no burning trash piles, and there's a Range Rover blocking the intersection, not a cow. Many of the people who live in Mendham work in New York City. I still don't really know what managing a hedge fund and lawyering look like but I watch them take the train into the city—clean-shaven, steely, and ready for a day of commerce. Once they step off the platform back home, they shed their suits and head to soccer practices, homework support, and family dinners. The last time I saw any hint of unrest was when some developer threatened to build a Dunkin' Donuts on East Main Street. Life is comfortable in Mendham. I worry that comfort will stand in the way of change. The world where five-year-olds work as stonemasons is far, far away, kept at a distance.

As we drive the last few feet of downtown, my mind spins like a clothes dryer, part of me wanting to stop and eat a bagel, and the other part of me wanting to get to work and scream, "Do you know what's going on in Nepal?!" at the top of my lungs.

Kopila Valley needs cash, and we need it fast. That's why I came back to New Jersey. In Surkhet, Daju and Bauju and their kids, BBC and Shova, are vigilantly watching over construction and pretty much giving me an update with every brick. The walls are going up, and you can see the spots where windows will be. Daju says that it's beautiful already, but Daju is the kind of person who finds a piece of art wherever he looks. There is still lots of work to do, and every day we can't afford cement is one more day a child who needs a home goes without one.

My first course of action is babysitting. Since it's summertime and school is out, my calendar fills up quickly. I spend Monday with the Wintz family, who'd just had a baby girl. My weekends are with the Leibolds and the Bartzaks. The Conellys book me for several days at a time, whenever they head out of town to their place on the lake. By August, I'm working twelve-hour days, six days a week, plus every Saturday evening. Life is a hazy blur of freckles, sunscreen, yogurt cups, sprinklers, and Liams and Taylors, and I've read *The Giving Tree* so many times I could perform it as a monologue at Carnegie Hall, which I'd absolutely be up for doing if it paid well.

The parents of Mendham, including my own, are wonderfully supportive of me, but I don't think they understand why I'm not at Vassar or Boston College like everybody else's kids. There are days when I don't really understand it either, and all I can do is tell myself, and anyone else who asks, about the day I met Hima. They slip me tips and always remember to ask how the house is coming along, and even though I'm pulling in eight hundred dollars most weeks, it always manages to be just enough for what we need. I get a dog-sitting gig when we need new tools. Bill and Linda pay me extra for staying late, and we can afford the gorgeous Nepali *sal* wood we're using to frame the windows. When I get fed up with my business plan, one of the CEOs I babysit for comes home after date night, full of Bordeaux and the exact guidance I need. At the end of every week, I total up my cash and send a wire transfer to Nepal. For a while, funding the construction is effortless.

———————

TOPE CALLS ON a Monday in the middle of September. The hammock in my parents' backyard is filled with leaves, and the warty heirloom pumpkins and mums from the market have quietly made their way onto people's stoops. Overnight, Mendham ditched its patriotic summer outfit for corn husks and bales of straw. I've been away from Surkhet for a whole season.

"Bad news," Tope says with a sigh. "The septic tank needs to be installed, and we need more iron to set the roof. We're going to need $2,200 at the very least this week, in addition to the regular payment for the laborers, bricks, and cement."

My mom is in the kitchen with me, eavesdropping and opening all the cabinets on a mad hunt for just the right coffee mug. She has a mountain of ceramic rejects, all lined up on the breakfast table. How does one family get so many mugs?

"Shit," I say to Tope.

"Shit," he agrees.

He's sent over every monthly paycheck from his job. My babysitting gigs have started to dwindle, kids are back in school, and the grown-ups are too tired from homework help for date night. Every single cent I have is already tied up in lumber and masonry, and we're nowhere near ready to open the doors to Kopila Valley. Doors are expensive; we don't have any yet.

"What do you think we should do, Maggie?"

We have to halt construction. I tell him I'll think of something, but my mind is tired and empty. We hang up and agree to talk in a few days.

I look at the table full of sad, old mugs, chipped and stained yellow like teeth.

"Is everything okay?" my mom asks. For as long as I can remember, she's been trying to read my thoughts.

I look at the mugs again. And it hits me.

"Mom, I need help. We're going to throw a garage sale. This weekend."

———

PEOPLE IN NEW Jersey love garage sales. Even in a classy suburb like Mendham, nobody, no matter how impressive the job title or shiny the sedan, seems to be above haggling with a stranger for a pair of used cross-country skis or a poster of Bruce Springsteen. Sure, it's a little homier than a black-tie gala, but the garage sale is our first fundraiser, and I'm excited. I spend Tuesday with a cardboard box, combing the basement and looking for anything my parents won't miss: silk scarves, lampshades, and old crocheted blankets buried in dust. Board games and clutter tumble noisily down from high-up shelves, and our dog, Sophie, starts barking and stamping her paws. Soon, my parents creak down the stairs and join me, foraging for table runners and bad sweaters.

"What about these?" says my dad, holding up a stack of *National Geographic* magazines and a wacky-looking wine decanter.

"And this!" my mom chimes in, food processor perilously balanced over her head like a trophy.

They laugh when Sophie runs off with some odd piece of inventory stuffed in her cheek and cry when a pair of baby shoes takes them back twenty-two years.

I miss Surkhet, but I'm having fun here. We all are. The house is warm, and the toilet works. I hear "I love you" every day, and we speak the same language. Two thousand dollars behind and seven thousand miles away from the hole in the ground where I offered my heart and some flowers on a tray to an earth goddess whose name I can barely pronounce. I'm torn and wondering if it's possible to belong to two places at once.

Our house empties quickly of snow pants and bad art, and unless I'm underestimating the value of Tae Bo VHS sets, we still don't have nearly enough sellable goods to make the money we need. Throwing a shaky Hail Mary, I summon the office printer from a long, long sleep and make flyers asking our neighbors for knickknacks they're willing to donate to the cause, stuffing them into any mailbox I find and hoping for the best.

First, a bunch of old serving dishes arrive. Then the Bon Jovi CDs. A box of rumpled hats shows up shortly afterward, followed by a leaky blue bean bag chair and a wig about the same color. Another thing about New Jersey—everyone has a lot of stuff. Moms on the way to school drop-off sprint up the driveway with slow cookers and teddy bears to add to the collection, and in the evening, they come by again with old books and slippers. By Friday morning, we're swimming in wonderful, magical, curious, totally sellable junk.

My older sister, Kate, comes home from college and bakes oatmeal cookies to sell while my youngest sister, Libby, eats spoonfuls of the batter and unfolds the card tables, which are also donated and also very much for sale. My parents get busy displaying random items and trying to form a cohesive design story from bedsheets, saltshakers, and old camping equipment. All huddled up in the garage together, air candied with vanilla extract, burnt sugar, and the sound of my dad's James Taylor CD, it feels like we're celebrating a holiday that only belongs to us.

I wonder how the hell I'll say goodbye again, to family, to this well-worn, love-drunk place of comfort where nothing has hurt before, and no one could ever be lonely. My breath slows, and I lose myself in a few verses of the music. Inevitably, through the singing and the smell of ground nutmeg, I remember Hima. I hear the *crack*, *crack*, *crack* of the rock breakers' tools as James Taylor sings to us about how sweet it is to be loved.

The early birds show up at six in the morning on Saturday and keep coming until dusk. The next day is the same. We barter the best we can, but you can only sell a used dog leash so hard while keeping a straight face. By the end of the weekend, strangely exhilarated and smelling like mothballs, I count all the money—every single nickel, penny, and dime. It totals $2,227, and it goes straight to Nepal.

Monday morning comes, and on the front page of the local paper is a photo of our house in Surkhet. Well, our *almost* house—four brick walls, cement, iron rods, and the tree that started it all. A kind reporter came by over the weekend to interview me about Kopila Valley (and scope out the garage sale, obviously), but I didn't expect it to be front-page news. The photo is giant, bigger than my head, colored brightly, still warm and stinking of ink. There's a smaller photo of me in the corner, too, standing on the driveway next to a velvet painting, smiling and doing a funny thing with my eye.

I read the headline:

"LOCAL TEEN HOSTS GARAGE SALE
TO BUILD NEPAL ORPHANAGE."

I cringe a little. Kopila Valley is not an orphanage; it's a *home*. At least it will be. We're not a stop on the way to finding a family; we *are* the family. The last thing I want to be is the feel-good story that dresses up the true story: children are suffering in this world, and we're failing them. I call Tope, grumbling about journalistic fluff, and he stops me.

"Listen," he says. "People need to know about the problem, but they also need to believe that they can be a part of the solution. Have faith, Maggie—this article could really be something."

And as always, he's right.

By Tuesday, the emails are coming in.

By Thursday, the first check arrives—five hundred dollars from the parents of a gal who was in my grade at high school.

Elderly couples put twenty-dollar bills in envelopes and drop them in the mailbox. Kindergartners empty their piggy banks into plastic bags and leave them at my parents' door. Suddenly, everybody in Mendham knows what's happening in Nepal. Even if they didn't know where Nepal was three days ago. The envelopes keep pouring in: five dollars, ten dollars, and fifteen dollars at a time for the next month. Then the larger checks begin to arrive.

An incredibly charismatic woman named Kim Wentworth takes me to lunch at the Black Horse Tavern (watching her eat a Cobb salad is just about the most glamorous thing I've ever seen). I'm amazed by her grace and her poise. At the end of the lunch, she tells me she notices a sparkle in my eye, tells me that she believes in me, and that she's going to match the five thousand dollars of babysitting money I'd invested in starting Kopila Valley. The next month, she invites me to a ladies' luncheon where I stand and tell my story of going to Nepal for the first time. Mike Seergy, who used to be the CEO of Nissan, tells me "he likes my hustle." He shines up my business plan, leads me through the rest of my paperwork like a lame pony, and agrees to serve on my board. Marjorie Keith, a huge-hearted mom in Mendham, writes a check from their family fund and gives me a pep talk and some advice on registering a nonprofit, which I need to do in order to accept the donations that will fund Kopila Valley. On a Friday, exhausted and bleary-eyed, I head to the Mendham post office where there's a sole envelope. I open it up and read a handwritten note from a woman named Amie Bloom. I remember her from the luncheon. Inside the envelope is a check for $20,000 in memory of Amie's late son. I fall to the floor against the wall of post boxes and land in a puddle of tears.

Weeks later, just before Christmas, a package from the IRS arrives, with our final 501(c)(3) approval notice. I decide to call our organization the BlinkNow Foundation. When I saw how children in Surkhet were living, my worldview changed in the blink of an eye. A child's life can transform in the blink of an eye. Everything is happening in the blink of an eye and shifting from "me" to "we."

It's early December when Priti Maheshwari, a teacher from the Red Oaks School in Morristown, calls. She leaves a message for me at the BlinkNow headquarters (currently located by the pots in my parents' kitchen) and asks if I'd be interested in coming to talk to her class about my work in Nepal. They found the *Observer*

Tribune piece when they were clipping articles about moral courage for a collage. *Moral courage.* My ego goes for a strut.

I've never talked to a group of young children before. All day long, I'm happy to profess the virtues of travel to high schoolers. I'm also happy to hit some business folks with the virtues of corporate social responsibility, but talking to kids is tough. Every conversation is one where innocence morphs into awareness and never quite returns to what it once was. Every kid sees a version of themselves in one of the slides from Nepal and learns in an instant that the wide, wonderful world holds misery alongside magic. The good news is that we can help—that's the real miracle in all of it.

I over-caffeinate and underprepare the day of the Red Oaks talk. Palm sweats and coffee jitters render my hands completely useless, and I have to shoulder-check the classroom door to open it. When I do stumble over the threshold, forty little faces framed by pigtails and mushroom cuts smile up at me and say hello, somehow at forty slightly different times. Giggly girls in pink erupt into full-blown laughter under a flurry of paper snowflakes. My heart stops for a second. They're about the same age as the girls who are living by the riverbed breaking rocks in Nepal, most at risk for trafficking and child marriage.

I get set up with my PowerPoint. The class hushes. Ms. Priti gives me a nod. All I can hear is the clock and a guinea pig drinking as politely as it can from the giant bottle in its cage. Hima's gorgeous face appears on the projector screen. The kids gasp and *ooh* and *ahh*.

"Does anybody know where Nepal is?" I ask, not expecting much.

"Nepal is located on the northeastern border of India," a boy, no more than nine, answers after clearing his throat.

"And what is Nepal famous for?" I counter. Fifteen hands pop up, all desperate to be chosen.

"Mount Ev-o-west!" a little girl shouts.

"Yetis!" shouts another.

"Anyone else know any interesting facts about Nepal?" I venture. Now I'm actively trying to stump them.

"Yes," a little boy answers from the back of the room. "It has a *very* different-shaped flag."

"Wow! You're right!" I'm bouncy and loud. Ms. Priti looks on proudly at her students.

"Okay, I have a favor to ask you guys." I get serious and sink down to the blue rug with them. "There's something I need your help with. I'll tell you about it, and then you can decide if you think you want to help. Deal?"

"Deal!" they cheer.

"Many children in Nepal don't get to go to school, and it makes them so sad. Many of them would do *anything* to go to a class just like this. How much do you think it costs to put a child in school in Nepal?"

"A thousand dollars?" the first child asks.

"No, but good guess," I say.

"Five hundred dollars," says the next one.

"Three hundred dollars," another ventures.

"Nope." I smile. "Lower."

They fall quiet, clearly done with my guessing game.

Fanning out my fingers, I give them the skinny. "Guys, it can cost as little as five dollars for an admission fee. What if I told you that everyone here today could send their own special friend in Nepal to school?"

They start to wiggle.

"All you need to do is decorate an ornament, pull a name out of this paper bag, and write your friend's name and age on the ornament. Then we're going to sell them."

Their eyes get big.

"Sound good?"

They smile and high-five me. The guinea pig's nose quivers nervously from the corner of his cage, and Ms. Priti shrinks near the doorway. She pops out and asks them to use their calm voices. We pass out glitter, glue, and sequins, and each child picks out a name.

"I want Jyoti!" cries one.

"I want Hima," pouts another.

"All of these children are special," I assure them, "and they all need our help."

A gentle snow falls outside the classroom window, as we cut and paste and sing the first few lines of "Rudolph the Red-Nosed Reindeer" over and over again. I watch the little brows furrow and soft, pudgy hands cut slow, careful shapes from craft paper. There are anthills of fine green glitter on the worktables, and everyone is sticking stickers to their shirts. When I was their age, it never crossed my mind that childhood was a luxury, that kids at the other end of the earth weren't doing exactly what I was doing, or some exotic version of it.

I take a break from trying to glue my angel's wing back on and look up at the photo of Hima. She's been grinning behind us, all zoomed-in and cheesy, the entire time. She's as real a child as the one scribbling away next to me, as worthy of love, safety, and opportunity. I wonder who I would have been if I'd known she was out there earlier. I wonder who these kids will be.

WITH BROWNISH BANKS of snow on the street, bulbs on the PVC tree, and Clark Griswold balancing on his rooftop, another Doyne Christmas comes and goes. The house in Surkhet is almost finished. We have just enough money to finish up the major stuff and buy my plane ticket, one-way, to Kathmandu. While packing a suitcase and about to fly away, I realize that Mendham is more home to me now than it ever has been; the little town that turned down Dunkin' Donuts opened its arms to Kopila Valley. Everything is beautiful here with landscaped promenades, kind families, and perfect white ducks swimming in the pond, deli sandwiches on rye with pickle spears, comfort and abundance. But it isn't my life anymore.

I say a long goodbye to New Jersey and get a much-needed haircut, Taylor egg, ham, and cheese from the Wicker Basket deli, and a visit to my friends at college. They ask me when I'm coming back and what I think I'll do with my life, and I give them the easiest answer I can: "I don't know."

As my friends and I walk through a shimmering, ice-covered quad, we're flanked by handsome brick buildings and people exactly like us. I imagine the life that would have been, the life that everyone expected of me: joining a sorority, playing lacrosse, getting good grades, drinking Jell-O shots and puking in the coed bathroom, getting a job, maybe meeting someone and falling in love. I mourn it, but I celebrate the birth of a life that feels true.

Guys play beer pong in one of the dorms, and my friends whisper about who's going home with whom. Jangly college rock plays, but I don't know the words to the songs. All the while, I hear the sound of the rock-breaking girls in the river.

4

HOMECOMING

Dear J,
I felt prepared to do the work and teach you all the things
you would need to learn.
  I had it wrong. It's you who has done the teaching.

  —M

B REATH IS THE first sound I hear in the morning. The tides of my own body, slow, tired, and steady, rise out from my nose in plumes and get lost in the shower of sunlight. Before BBC wakes up, before the scrape of wet cement on the edge of a trowel, after the choir of neighborhood dogs ends their twelve-hour nightly chorale performance, home is a quiet feeling that arrives even before I can remember where I am. I get up slowly and walk the hallways. I stick my head in the rooms where, someday soon, children will sleep, and I place my hands on the cold, scaly cement walls. I swear I can feel a pulse, a promise of the life that will be here.

A far-off rooster crows itself awake, and BBC's three-year-old feet beat against the floor. Shova wakes up as though she's in the middle of a conversation and giggles sweetly at her brother. Soon Kopila Valley will be full of twice the amount of noise and tears and chatter. I smile, my first smile of the day, knowing that home will not be a quiet feeling for long.

The house is still a construction site. There are ten of us sleeping in two small rooms, one of which also serves as a makeshift kitchen: Daju; Bauju; their kids Shova and BBC; their nephew Birendra; our mason Chiran; and his lovely wife, Guineau, who is also helping with the construction. Their two daughters are also staying on-site. During the day, there's a rotating cast of masons, laborers, neighbors, and me. I don't need to learn names in Nepal; everyone is "brother," "sister," "auntie," or "uncle." We have no electricity and no water—not even glass in the windows to keep January outdoors where she belongs. I wear a fleece jacket, mittens, and a gaiter to bed to keep warm, but my face chaps anyway, making me extremely pink and difficult to take seriously. All of my belongings fit into a sad, dented, rusty, paint-chipped tin box that some happy cockroaches have made their way inside. I rotate through a few kurtas (Nepali tops that are long) with big, rounded Punjabi pants, but I don't go all out with saris and deutis and nose jewelry like the true locals. I feel obligated to do what I can to fit in. Shorts and tank tops are a thing of the past, and I embrace the modesty the culture asks for. Kurta sural is a good middle ground, but I'm finding that most of mine are now covered in paint and wood stain, proof of living and breathing on a construction site.

The other things in my box are my Nepali books. Slowly and surely, I'm starting to string words together. I keep a journal and a pledge to myself to learn ten words a day and build a vocabulary. The majority of my vocabulary at the moment focuses on construction words: *Eeta* means "bricks." *Falum* is "iron." Lucky for me, some of the words translate over. *Cement-i* is "cement."

Everything is moving in Nepali time, but there's a sweetness to it that I couldn't stomach rushing if I wanted to. The small fireplace we decided to put in at the last minute becomes the center of our universe. In the daytime, it crackles and spits and warms our tea while we're busy painting the walls the color of buttermilk. BBC plays in a giant cardboard box and makes all of us stop what we're doing to laugh, even the busy masons. In the evenings, Bauju cooks corn roti and bitter greens effortlessly over the big orange flame and makes me feel about as self-sufficient as a baby kangaroo. Sometimes she makes popcorn, dumping it straight from the pot onto the mortar-covered floor for us to eat. We sing songs, and I study my Nepali: counting to ten—"*ek, dui, tin, char, panch, cha, saat, aath, nau, das*"—over and over again until BBC and Shova doze off in a heap, shadow and light flickering across their backs. I can't understand much of what the construction crew says to me, but I think we're somewhere between four days and four months behind schedule.

There is so much about life here that I don't yet understand, but plenty that I do. There are children everywhere in our neighborhood. They run at me in masses on my daily walk, bare feet thundering in the dirt, just a big cloud of dust that passes over, screaming, "Hi! Hi! Hi! Hiiiii!" They are tightly coiled springs that seem to burst open in all directions the second they see me, darting about, collapsing with belly laughs, and leaping up, lungs magically full of breath again. I'm allowed to be a bystander for about three seconds before I'm pulled in one direction or another for a neighborhood game of tag or soccer, claimed by one team or another. I thank God that the rules of play defy the rules of language, that childhood can be our common tongue:

I kick the ball to you; you kick it back to me.

You find a ladybug, and I let you set it on the top of my hand so I can fawn over its perfectly placed spots.

I never tell them this, but they're excellent teachers. By February, my Nepali is less garbled, and their English is getting good too. The kids can say, "Hi! How are you?" and "What is your name?" and I can reply, "*Mero nam Maggie ho*" ("My name is Maggie"). I go to visit Hima and her family in the evenings, and the children always drop whatever ball or toad they have in their hands and shout, "Good morning, Maggie!" That one I can't bear to correct.

While we work with the local government and child welfare officers and social workers on making our home base an official permanent placement facility for children, we focus our other efforts on outreach, drawing a small circle around the dry riverbed and chipping away at school enrollment. We enroll thirty children in school and collaborate with the local Marie Stopes clinic to make family planning more accessible to impoverished families and rural communities. The realities of globalism are starting to hit Nepal: everyone wants to learn English and I begin teaching a free English language class on the big, flat roof of the house.

Fifteen kids show up on the first day. I've been working on the construction site all day and I don't have anything planned out. We stare at each other in complete silence for a full minute before I can say anything at all. Shova is looking horrified, a little bit for me and a little bit for herself, and shoots me a thumbs-up from the back.

In Nepali and English, I'm most confident talking about food, so that's where I start. Before I can stop myself, I'm singing and dancing and miming like some awful plainclothes birthday clown.

"Making roti! Making roti!" I channel Bauju and pat imaginary dough with the palm of my hand.

The kids look up at me. I don't blame them for being suspicious. Sweat gathers on my neck and shoots down my backbone, as I think back to the brief English as a Second Language course I took during my time in the States.

"What do you make roti with? Your *hands*! Look, these are my *hands*. Clap your hands!"

I *clap, clap, clap*, and they do the same in the strange, syncopated rhythm of pure confusion.

"After you make roti, what do you have to do? Wash your *hands*!" I rub my hands together under an imaginary faucet. They follow.

Suddenly, BBC hops up and starts singing along with me, a kindness he's too young to understand. It takes approximately four seconds for the other fourteen kids to join him. They shake their bony butts, slap their hands together, and knead their invisible dough like it's the last thing they'll do.

"Making roti, wash your hands. Making roti, wash your hands. Everybody! Clap your hands!" *Clap-clap, clap-clap, clap-clap!* It sounds like the beat of the Cha Cha Slide.

"Making Roti, Wash Your Hands" is an instant hit in Surkhet.

On the second day, thirty kids show up.

On the third, forty-five. The rooftop of our new home is at capacity. The kites soar overhead, and we sing songs together as the sun sets across the golden wheat paddies and over the foothills.

———

UNLIKE THE SLOW-MOVING river, gossip rushes through Surkhet, eddying at the market and near the shops, drenching the porters and elders, and flooding the bus park. We're opening a home for children, and once word spreads that we're here to help, people come to us in droves. They huddle near the edge of the property.

They bang on the door, sometimes sobbing or yelling what can only be expletives. Orphans arrive at the advice of relatives who can't afford to care for them, derelict and filthy, wrapping their arms around me and refusing to let go. Others stand mute on the stoop, empty-eyed and visibly broken, with their hands cupped to receive whatever is offered to them—rice, water, money. There are trash pickers and domestic servants as young as six, widows and battered women looking for a place to hide until their husbands drink themselves to death. They wander in one by one and I try to take time for each of them. I can only pick up bits of Nepali so I rely on a translator, and my new Nepali tutor Chetana.

We can't help everybody. Tope reminds me of this every single morning when I call him, trying the best I can to disguise the fact that I'm a complete mess, that I've spent all night rolling around in my sweat, consumed by sad stories. That the responsibility of helping is too much. That I'm idealistic and naive.

The crowds form in the morning. Daju and Bauju try their best to get information from patiently sifting through the hundreds of tragedies. We need paperwork to verify income, age, and disability. We need birth certificates to enroll children in school. The idea that the documentation exists is laughable. Many of the relatives of children we meet have no idea how old their children are, only that they were born during the monsoon season. Many of the sick have never seen a doctor before; they only know that the ginger and herbs the village shaman or ayurvedic healers prescribed didn't make them better.

I do my best to discriminate between the poor and the desperate, the hungry and the starving, who we can help and who is beyond help. I learn to rely on the local community who know more than I do. The probability that I get it wrong is a ghost I expect to haunt me forever. People die here; they get ill, often without fanfare. Life comes and goes. Grief is something you carry with you or leave behind. It doesn't seem to stop anybody. Except me.

———————

SOMETIMES, DECIDING WHO to assist takes months. Other times, it only takes an instant. One day, on my way to get bananas from the fruit stand, I find a boy completely unconscious on the road. Apart from the body on the ground collecting curious flies, it's a beautiful day. The air is warm for winter. The streets are full of shoppers heading to market, but nobody stops for the boy. Nobody even seems to notice him. There are lots of street children here. They're a part of the scenery. Sometimes they come to us at the house for food, but many of them have been surviving for so long that they don't seem to need or want us. A woman steps over him with the same motion as someone stepping over a puddle. I watch as she keeps walking toward the produce stall. Maybe when you're a citizen of this world, you instinctively know who can be helped and who can't. Maybe you're too busy looking for help of your own.

As I approach him, lying there on the road, I can see that his body is covered in scabies, tiny mites that burrow under the skin that are hated for their persistence. He's alive, but barely, by the look of it. His ribs swell and fall ever so slightly as I crouch down and try to lift him, lice crawling from his skin to mine with an unmistakable tickle. He weighs as much as an alley cat, and his lips are cracked and dry like a stretch of desert.

Who are you? I wonder, even though I know these questions can be impossible to answer.

A weak, fluttery pulse taps away under the corner of his jaw, and his shorts are soaked with urine. I need to get him to a hospital.

Streets spin, and smells drift in and out of my nose—chai and piss and hot food—as I run in all the wrong directions to the local medical clinic, navigating with nothing but instinct. My legs feel like spaghetti noodles, and I don't know where I am or where I need to go, in so, so many ways. I pass the jewelry shops and the market and the King Birendra statue, but nobody seems to notice us. I pass the butcher where the goats scream and the tiny bank. Eventually, after stopping and spinning and looking absolutely frantic, people begin to point us in the right direction. I let the warmth of his skin against mine comfort me enough to keep going.

We arrive at the hospital, and the ER is a boiler room. Ants crawl freely in and out of the doorway in an endless black column, a few veering out of formation to drown themselves in a pool of blood-laced fluid. A woman with a gash on her head slumps over in the corner, rousing only to vomit on herself and her little daughter, and a sullen thousand-year-old man with no legs glares at me from his wheelchair. The nurses seem bored and unconcerned. They let their eyes pause on the boy and decide to move on to somebody else. Then somebody else after. After an hour, his skin starts to turn yellowish and his breathing slows, so I start to yell.

"*Malaai sahayog chaiyo!*" ("I need help!")

I shove the boy at them.

"Look! Look at him!"

In an instant, I feel hysterical sorrow, the grief of every single man, woman, and child who has come to Kopila Valley and begged for help.

But you can't help everyone.

Thankfully, the nurses take the boy from me, and a student who speaks English comes over to apologize for the wait. They've seen the boy before, and he promises that they'll help him. He says there is only one doctor here. They do their best. In our entire district, there are only five doctors in total, constantly rotating from Kathmandu and Nepal Ganj.

I do the math.

One doctor. Just one, to serve a town of 28,000 and a district of 100,000 people, plus the mountain districts with a few hundred thousand more.

I thank the doctor, collect my things, and leave the boy with the doctor, even though it hurts me. I don't know where he'll go after this or what will happen. The house is almost done, but I'm not qualified to care for him. I don't know if he has a family, and there are no documents. His case doesn't fit the criteria. He doesn't fit the criteria.

Sun long gone, I start off toward the house, listening to the sweet old song that the crickets seem to sing no matter where in the world they are. I pick up my grief and my guilt, and I carry it home.

———

IN A FEW weeks, the weather begins to get warmer, the days lengthen, and winter assures us it will be leaving soon. The country is still in turmoil. Political uprisings have begun to crop up in the mountains again, and everything from healthcare to the roads is unreliable. Lots of children were recruited by the Maoists during the civil war, so keeping them safe feels especially urgent. The first floor of the house is completely finished, and we're ready to begin taking in children.

The first child who comes to stay with us is Nisha. She lives in a cluster of mud huts on a hillside about an hour and half from Surkhet. The daughter of a community elder told me about her, and one of the doctors from the Marie Stopes clinic agrees to drive me out on his motorbike to see her. Nisha has no family. Her mother died of ovarian cancer, and her father drank himself to liver failure six months later. Her two older half-siblings are long gone, laborers in India or maybe the Middle East; nobody seems quite sure. A neighbor took her in after her mother's death. Nisha's been watching the neighbors' young children and animals in exchange for food.

After asking around and explaining who we are, we locate the little hut where Nisha is.

"Namaste, bahini," we call softly to her and wait. Warily, she leaves the dark, one-room home and steps out into the bright winter light.

She's small, maybe five or six years old, with short, choppy hair and a tiny stick in her nose for a pin. Her face is round and healthy, which is a relief, and she has freckles like perfect constellations on her cheeks. Shivering, she tugs the thin red shawl around her shoulders and bounces a whimpering baby on her back.

I let the doctor do most of the talking, and I watch for nods and frowns. He asks Nisha if she's interested in going to school and living in a home with other kids, and her chin bobs up and down. She ducks inside the hut to set the baby down, and comes out, ready to go. I smile, half-excited and half-heartbroken that a child could leave everything they've ever known so easily. The family she's been living with eagerly accepts our offer, maybe because they genuinely want a better life for her, or maybe because, at five years old, she isn't much help anyway.

It takes us just a week to get her birth certificate, and she arrives on February 12, 2008, the night before her sixth birthday. She moves into a room with Shova, who immediately begins calling her "sister" and braiding her hair. Nisha is smart and responsible; she teaches herself how to read late into the night and takes the chance to go to school seriously.

After Nisha come Sagar and Goma, a brother-sister duo I hear of from my Nepali tutor. Both of their parents have passed, and they've been living with an abusive uncle. They sell peanuts by the bus park to get by. When they come to live at the house, there's never more than an inch of space between them. At seven and five years old, the only safety in their lives has been their proximity to each other. I don't think they knew how to live any other way. Even after a few weeks, they flinch when we touch them and curl into each other even tighter. I don't know that one would have survived the years of abuse without the other.

We're selective about the kids we take in. We have to be. Our resources are limited, our space is limited, and I'm still learning the language. As a rule, we don't take children who have living family members or relatives capable of caring for them. We don't separate siblings. We don't take medically fragile children we're unqualified to treat. If a child doesn't want to live at Kopila Valley, we don't try to convince them. In general, development best practices are to keep children with their biological family if and whenever possible. We're quick to turn down families who are looking to hand their kids over, which, sadly, are about 99 percent of cases that come our way. These families need counseling about their options—often a scholarship or food support and best of all employment. We give them what we can and try to show them that we're not the path to a better life for their children. *They* are.

Cases come our way from village committees, INGOs (international NGOs), the police, and officers throughout different government branches. Each one has to be carefully vetted. We trek to villages, gather information and paperwork, and learn to not trust everything we read or hear. I try to remember and record anecdotes and check stories. We have to be sure that even government officials aren't referring a distant relative and to comb through supportive documents and police files. Social workers, neighbors, and the board of locals Tope and I have put together all step up to help review cases, but still I struggle to know what's true and what's just designed to seem that way. Even though there seem to be more rules in cricket than in adoption here, we insist on filing all of the legal paperwork and working with the government officers assigned to the ministry of child welfare in our regional office. For the children who do come under our care, we make every attempt to keep strong records and connections with villages and root families so that our children can stay connected to where they come from long into the future.

In the spring, Krishna Shahi comes to live with us, bringing all the sunshine in the world. Then Pankha, who brings all the mischief. Krishna Bogati, our little comedian and performer, arrives in May, followed by Bhakta, who doesn't say a word.

None of the children have ever lived in a house like Kopila before, so the transition is not graceful. They flick the lights on, off, on, off, on, off, for hours, and they don't trust the toilet. They almost scowl at it when they walk by the bathroom, and I'm constantly looking out the window to find somebody squatting in the side yard. They use the tables as chairs and the chairs as tables, and they drop their fruit peels on the floor, expecting that some secret goat will wander into the house and eat them. For a month, we have six bedwetters at one time. The sheets and wool-stuffed mattresses are soaked all the way down to the plywood slats in the morning, and since the kids all sleep together, others are covered in pee too. Someone is always sick. Chicken pox hits. Then viral fevers. Then diarrhea so furious that more than once I find *myself* squatting in the side yard. The water can't be trusted. It only comes on between two and four in the morning, so we have to wake up and fill buckets and tanks for the day. It randomly spurts out of the spigot in the middle of the afternoon, looking like contaminated brown pudding. Somebody comes out to fix it, we splurge on our first water filter, and the diarrhea clears up shortly afterward.

Loving children is easy. Caring for them is harder than anything I could have imagined. I can give them food and beds and education. I can sing songs and play games. I can walk them to school and wash their clothing. But when I hear cries of "Amma!"—cries for their own mothers—ricocheting off the walls at two in the morning or fighting their way out of pink, feverish cheeks, I can't answer the call the way they want me to. I go through the motions of mothering in earnest, but I can't bring their mothers back. All I can do is try my best to love them through grief and trauma so intense and so wretched that my wildest attempts to conceive of it in my mind are still a million miles away from knowing.

In the refuge of daytime, tucked in, buttoned up, lunches in hand, big grins on little faces, you would never know that these kids had faced a single disappointment in life, but they seem to sink with the sun, in the most tender, precious moments of the day. I kiss them goodnight and watch their lashes fall together. I leave them in what I think is peace. But an hour later, I hear soft whimpers in the air.

By summer, our days ease into rhythm with the monsoon rains slapping against the roof. We wake up in the mornings, brush our teeth, do chores, and then make our way outside for morning tea in the sun and a game of marbles in the side yard. Daju buys a little bell that we bang on with a spoon for meals. We get the kids ready for school and drop them off. I send emails, review cases, go to the market, and come home again when school is out. Between me, Ubji, Bauju, Daju, and Tope in India, everything feels under control. The kids in the house are thriving, and with the promise of tiffin (school snack), even the wariest students in the scholarship program are finally showing up to class. Still, I feel unsettled, unsure about what or who will come next, but the constant current of anxiety is something I get used to, along with sleeplessness, wild hair, and the other trappings of parenthood.

I miss my own parents madly, and it feels strange not to have them near as we sign adoption papers, celebrate birthdays, and set off in the mornings for school. Even stranger and lonelier are the times when our community loses someone, when I don't know what to do, when I have to turn a mother away. Graciously, the mountains seem to watch over me while I watch over the children, gentle, green giants that make sure I don't unravel completely when somebody throws up for the seventh time or when we almost run out of money. I look to them for comfort at the end of a hard day, foliage drunk and obnoxiously green, leaves so lush and waxy I can see my face in them. They remind without a word that so much is a season. The air will dry. The branches will thin. The birds and bugs will quiet for a time. We fall into our rhythms, and one day, rhythms change.

5

MOONSTAR

Dear N,
The reason I'm so in love with your smile is because I can
see through to how big and bright your heart is.

—M

CHILDREN TOUGHEN YOU in a way nothing else can. The woman I was when I trekked to Oda in 2008 is different from the one who quivered up the mountain two years ago. A full day on the Nepali bus can't turn my stomach anymore. Maha Bua, just as steep and jagged as it was before, doesn't look as tall. I don't flinch when a shepherd sends his manic goats around a corner and straight into me. My own body remembers to hug the side of the mountain and wait with even breath until the smear of brown fur and mud passes by. At night, I lay my head in the dirt and fall asleep easily, while the mountain dogs yodel into the void. I trust myself as I would a friend, maybe for the first time ever.

We've been getting lots of case referrals from Dhailek, Jumla, and Kalikot, three mountain districts to the north where the civil war had its strongest foothold, and I want to come and see the places and the people with my own eyes. Tope and I had also promised a new tin roof to a school in the area, which would get students back in the building and learning. I want to be there when it happens. I want to visit Oda again as well, as I promised I would.

For two days, from sunrise to sunset, I hike the mountains, stopping to drink sweet spring water from my hands and eat hot meals in village homes, this time knowing what to say and how to act as a guest. It feels good to be a guest. Nobody is asking me for papaya or another game of marbles. I miss the kids, but they prepared me well for a reunion with the quiet, and I know that they're in good hands with Daju and Bauju, the stronger half of the parenting team.

Oda appears exactly as it did last time, a shimmering green gem tucked carefully between the mountain and the sky. From the crest of a hill, the homes are almost indiscernible from the boulders and piles of brown rock. It's a fairy garden forever lost if you don't know where to look. By the time I reach the edge of the village, there are kids piling on my back, and I'm welcomed with so much love and ruby-colored tikka that I look like a lobster before I can even set my bag down. The village aunties hold my face in their hands and tell me how fat I look, a normal and lovely thing to say in Nepal. Sunita's relatives claim me quickly, and their little boy takes my bag and lugs it into their mud house, where we sing, share stories, and wait for the hoarse whisper of the fading fire to lull us to sleep. After too many buckwheat pancakes and a cup of *raksi* (which is basically Nepali moonshine), I sleep deeply and more peacefully than I have in months.

———

JUST AFTER DAWN, pink, sweaty, and wearing the clothes I slept in, I wander through the labyrinth of homes to get some air, down to the glen where the sheep graze. The mountains can get cold at night, but as soon as the morning sun hits, a mud hut is like the inside of a potbellied stove.

The path is worn by millions of hooves and hundreds of journeys, slicing through tall, thick grass and over a large hump of meadow. The footing is solid as rock and worn totally, permanently bald. Closing my eyes, I listen to the sound of fifty churning sheep jaws at work and watch the large wooly forms beginning to take shape in the mist. They look as much like clouds as the clouds do.

A little girl looks up at the snowcapped mountains and sings to them in the sweetest voice.

"Namaste." I wave at her. These three days are the longest I've been away from the kids, and my world feels somewhat eerie without everlasting games of UNO and bedtime stories.

The girl turns sharply, startled. After a pause, she comes toward me at a timid shuffle. It's clear that I've interrupted something, but she doesn't seem upset.

When she gets closer, my face drains of blood and my lungs fill in an instant. Her left eye is as big as my fist, and the lid is stretched so far back into itself that she could only dream of closing it. She does everything she can do to hide it behind the thick hair that falls like a raven's wings over her face. I try not to stare but fail. It's like nothing I've ever seen before.

"It really hurts," she tells me in Nepali. "I can't see."

"I'm sorry," I tell her. "It looks painful."

Her name is Juntara, which she tells me means "Moonstar." I don't know what else to do but hold her hands and listen to her sing while the sheep bleat. I can imagine and hear the taunting and the teasing, and I can almost feel my own eye bursting from my skin. The deformity is so severe that she looks like a monster cyclops. I hate to admit it, but I find her hard to look at.

What is this?

How does it happen?

Can it be fixed?

My brain is on fire, roaring at me the same way it was when I met Hima.

What if we took her to the hospital?

Is it a tumor?

Can her vision be restored?

———

JUNTARA AND I spend the next few afternoons sitting together outside of her hut and sheep-gazing. There are cliffs and steep rocks everywhere, and the blindness has made her virtually immobile. She tells me about the cool water that runs in the creek, the delicious, bittersweet walnuts that fall down from the trees in fall, and her family's animals, mostly buffalo and a few goats. She sings the most beautiful, mournful songs, and her small voice becomes enormous in the echoey Himalayan amphitheater. Sometimes she really goes for it, like a miniature Nepali Celine Dion.

I don't want to upset her, so I don't ask much about the eye. I'm terrified that if she *does* cry, something terrible might happen. I wait and listen, picking up bits of information as we weave between sheep and skip stones on the river: It started five years ago, she can't see anything except flashes of light, and she's never seen a doctor. There are no doctors in Oda. There are no doctors *near* Oda. She spends most of her time inside her family's mud house, singing songs. There is talk that she is cursed. Superstition is common here.

I ask her about friends, and she replies, "I don't have many left."

"Juntara, I am your friend," I insist. A smile forms on her face. I know right then, without a doubt, that we need to do something.

The night before I leave Oda, I meet with Juntara's parents—a shy, thin man named Padam, and her mother, whose name I can't yet pronounce well. I tell them, maybe foolishly, that if they like, I can try to help their daughter. They say that they would like that very much.

———

WHEN I GET back to Surkhet, the kids are wild and muddy, leaping onto me before I can make it up the driveway.

"Did you see a wolf?" asks Goma.

"Did you see a snow leopard?" asks BBC.

"No," I say as I smile, "but I saw lots of sheep, and I made a new friend."

They want to know all about Juntara.

"What's her favorite color?"

"Does she have any sisters?"

"Is she big or little?"

"She has a very sick eye, and it makes her sad. We're going to try to help her."

They all agree that this is the best course of action and scamper off to bed. I open my computer and start researching right away. I call Tope and lay out the plan.

Things with Juntara's case move fast. I write an email with photos to our board in New Jersey and contact an organization in London called Facing the World, who fight for children with facial differences and provide care at no cost to the families. BlinkNow doesn't have the resources to help. Even with the donations from

Mendham, we're barely getting by, and we definitely don't have any doctors on staff. I send them pictures of Juntara, smiling big inside her family's mud house, playing by the river, looking up at the sky, hoping for the best but expecting nothing. Within days, they agree to look into her case. But, of course, they need more information.

We arrange for Juntara to come stay with us at Kopila Valley right away and set up a lifetime of doctor's appointments. The kids fall hard for her, fawning and fighting over her attention and wanting to learn all the songs from her village. I fall pretty hard for her, too, as we travel and talk. We go everywhere: to Nepalgunj for an MRI, Lucknow for CT scans, Kathmandu for a host of other imaging appointments. The trust she has in me is humbling. She gets on the bus for the first time, looks at her reflection in the glass windows, eats her first piece of candy. I send everything to London from the tiny post office in Surkhet and pray it will find its way there.

In August, less than a month later, I get an urgent email from Facing the World. The doctors want to operate as soon as possible. There's a tumor, and it's very serious because of the pressure it's putting on her optic nerve. They need to save whatever vision she has left.

They agree to write letters to the embassy to secure an emergency visa, and I agree to track down the necessary paperwork, *if* any paperwork exists. I practically run to Oda in a sweaty panic.

When I arrive, Juntara's family is sitting around a hissing fire that barely lights their hut. Her father, gentle as I remember, offers me some buckwheat porridge. Her mother tosses a few small sticks into the embers, which does nothing but release a stiff-tasting tuft of smoke. In my broken, stressed-out Nepali, I try to explain how serious the surgery is, how much time it will take, where they will need to go, and how they will get there. I tell them that Juntara could easily die during the operation. This doesn't seem to upset them. Death is different in a place where there are so few ways to prevent it, where there are landslides and leopards and no doctors. Health seems almost detached from mortality.

Juntara herself seems too young to feel the gravity of the decisions being laid out before her. She's excited to go on a big adventure to England—all of the people she'll meet, the names she'll remember, the newness of it all. More than anything else, though, more than saving her vision or dulling the pain, she's excited to come back home after the trip and show her new face to everyone in her village.

"They'll all say, 'Before, your eye was so big, and now it's small.' They'll think I'm nice again." She pauses a moment and smiles.

"The doctor says that maybe I'll live and maybe I'll die, right?"

"Well, yes, but you have a much, much, *much* greater chance of living. And me, I know you'll live because I know how strong you are." I squeeze her hands. They're much steadier than mine are.

"Yes, I am strong," she says. And so, the odyssey begins.

First, we get the papers together, which is a flaming hot disaster. Nobody knows whether Juntara is nine or ten years old, whether she was born during the wheat harvesting month or the rice harvesting month. We guess the best we can. The district office has never processed a passport for a child before, and everyone is confused. One guy is convinced it's illegal. Eventually, exhausted by me, they give in. Juntara, Padam, and I head to Kathmandu for more imaging, the British embassy in Delhi for a visa, and then Indira Gandhi Airport to say goodbye.

———

"MAGGIE DIDI, I don't want to go without you. I'm gonna get lost."

Juntara is crying into my arms near the ticket counter. She's wearing her new blue jeans, sneakers, a fuzzy green sweater, and a pink jacket with a pink hat. I've packed her bag with cookies and peanuts, trail mix, chewing gum, apples, and dried coconut. Juntara and Padam have everything they could possibly need— enough snacks to walk to England. Padam is pacing, itchy and nervous and missing the mountains already.

"I wouldn't let you go if I thought you were going to get lost. There will be so many people to help you there. I have to get back to Nepal now," I tell her. It makes her cry harder.

The British Airways agent motions for us to come forward, and all my nerves come out in a jittery string of demands.

"Sir, please have one of your people guide them through customs and security. I've booked a wheelchair."

"Yes, yes, ma'am," he assures me.

"Sir, you'll have someone fill out all their forms?"

"Yes, of course. We're sending two of our staff with them." He exhales.

"Sir, they'll put them directly onto the airplane?"

As kindly as he can, he says, "Yes, you've booked a wheelchair. Our people can't leave them until they're on the airplane in their seats. Ma'am, this isn't the first time we've done this."

Obviously, though, it's my first time.

He looks over at Juntara and her father and smiles sympathetically at them.

They have enormous, bright red, laminated name tags tied to lanyards around their necks. There are "Help Me" signs pinned to their backs with their full names, photographs, an emergency contact number, flight information, and a message:

> Please help us. We are on our way to the UK for emergency medical treatment. We speak Nepali and cannot read or write. Sarah Driver-Jowitt of Facing the World will be waiting for us in London Heathrow.

Two agents arrive with the wheelchair, and we get Juntara settled.

"There are so many people here to help you, so many people to take you to the airplane. You'll do great. You're all set. I'll miss you. I love you," I say.

I can't stop touching her cheeks.

She's crying. I'm crying. Padam is crying. He's terrified for his daughter. Terrified to leave his buffalo and his goats for so long. Terrified to get on an airplane. He's never even seen a bicycle before.

I grab his hands. "Everything is going to be fine."

He nods at me with so much hope and fear and trust that I could buckle under it, and they walk away with their escorts, past the roti stand, the security line, and a giant Indian guard with a curly mustache. Padam's Nepali *topi* hat gets smaller and smaller, until it disappears completely.

A few days later, I get a call from Sarah, our contact at Facing the World, and like everyone who comes into contact with Juntara, she's absolutely smitten.

"This is the best kid in the world," she tells me. "That's what makes this news so devastating."

The doctors found a tiny bump on Juntara's forehead, right above her left eye, an alarming sign of something called neurofibromatosis type 2, a condition that causes tumors to grow along the nerves. They also discovered that the damage done to her optic nerve is permanent and impossible to restore. The tumors in her brain are widespread, and the long-term prognosis is not good, especially in rural Nepal without regular care. The doctor won't give up, and they have a plan. The first surgery will be to remove the bulk of the tumor around her eye. Then they'll address a mass in her ear and one at the base of her skull. Then they'll remove a lesion found on her spine. The procedures and healing will take several months, and even after that, they're not sure whether much will change. She'll need a lifetime of care and sophisticated treatment.

"Is she okay?" I ask.

"Yes," Sarah replies. I can hear the smile in her voice. "She's wonderful."

Juntara is happy. She's talking and singing and living in her flat in Chelsea like a proper aristocrat. There's a Nepali restaurant providing her and Padam with delicious, familiar meals, and they have a translator named Raj checking in on them several times a day.

Winter comes swiftly to Surkhet, and the green mountains wear sparkling snowy crowns. Juntara's first surgeries have gone perfectly. Her face is swollen, but her eye is completely level with her face. She's thriving. Padam is struggling though. He's been having what sound like panic attacks and says that if he stays in London, he'll choke and die. He's sick and dizzy, worried about his home and his buffalo. He can't stomach the sight of a sky with no mountains in it and has gone days without food. Sleep is fleeting. He can't sleep with the sound of the buses at night. In January, he begs to go back to Nepal. Since he's showing signs of serious mental distress, we book him a flight back to Nepal as soon as possible. I travel to London to oversee Juntara's second operation, which will remove the tumors in her brain.

Juntara is the best roommate I've ever had. Her favorite thing about our flat is the bathtub, which she refers to as our *"tato pokari"* or "hot lake," and she usually spends about an hour in there every day, splashing and singing away. Most people who meet her can't believe that she's blind. She's social, self-sufficient, and absolutely in love with her new friends and teachers. There's her translator, Raj; Sarah from Facing the World; and Nicolas from the French bakery downstairs, who brings us pastries every day. Everyone Juntara meets falls in love with her, and in a matter of weeks, we have our own small troop in London.

The Kopila kids send videos to her and want to know when they'll get to visit. The very idea of a double-decker bus fills their bellies with laughter, but they can't understand why everyone is so excited about the giant clock. Juntara doesn't understand either. She has friends now, and she's glowing.

It's amazing to see how alive she feels without pain. Even though she can't see, she's memorized the layout of the apartment and can navigate upstairs, downstairs, and to the toilet, without any help at all. We spend lots of our time cooking. Juntara will go into the cabinet, take out the potatoes, tomatoes, onion, and garlic, chop them all up on the cutting board, fill the pot with water and add the rice, set the table, and do the dishes. I help, too, when she lets me.

At night, the buses keep me awake, but I'm happy to stay up imagining the woman that Juntara will become. She's tenacious and brave, peaceful and wise, disarmingly kind. I look up at the ceiling, a habit I can't ever seem to quit, and it's like the last six months are projected on a flat white screen: walking through Kalikot, drinking tea in her mud house, checking my email obsessively, MRIs, visa offices, technicolor rickshaw rides through Delhi, cooking dahl in our kitchen. I drift off in the early morning, when I've run out of tales to tell myself. Everything feels right and worth it; everything is exactly as it should be.

In February, we learn that Juntara needs to have a third surgery. I go back to Nepal to take a breath before the next procedure, update Padam on Juntara's condition, and celebrate the Shivaratri holiday with the kids. On Shivaratri, you go to the temple for a pooja and to eat something called *bong prassad*, which supposedly gives you the strength of the Lord Shiva. It turns out that bong prassad is mostly made of marijuana. The children are devastated when I tell them that they can't have any.

While I'm away, my sister Kate flies to London to stay with Juntara. I can't think of anybody better to watch over her than the older sister who watched over me. Every few nights, we Skype with them and sing songs over the computer. Padam comes to visit so that he can see her too. He brings Nepali lemons and a bag of the walnuts she loves so much and promises to pass them on.

"Thank you, chori," Padam says to me in his low, quiet voice.

"She's doing so well," I tell him. "Soon you'll be able to see her in person."

I ARRIVE BACK in London in time for the third surgery, and it goes remarkably well. The doctors operate for nine hours, and I get to touch one of her little feet while she's sedated in the ICU. Kate and I take turns crying from the relief and staring in at her blissful slumber. Then, on March 4, 2009 at 4:30 p.m., her brain swells.

Out of nowhere, machines start beeping at us. Juntara falls in and out of consciousness. The doctors come running and rush her off to surgery again. They work for hours, trying to put a shunt in, but it's too late. Kate and I sit by the bed, shattered. We hold her through her last breaths as the life support machines slow, as her lungs and heart stop. We are shocked; we can't move. We can't speak, and for a moment it feels like we'll stop breathing too. We did everything right. The doctors did everything right. I watched her fill with life, joy, and strength. Then I watched all of it leave her.

We contact her family through an army base camp near her village and carry out their wishes for a traditional Hindu burial. Then we go back home to the green valley, the cool water, the walnut trees, without the person who belongs there most of all. We bring her belongings back to Oda. Padam sobs quietly, and I see Juntara's face in his for the very first time.

Kate goes home heartbroken, and the kids go back to school, but for me, there's no closure. I live in a house with orphans. Their lives have been shaped by loss, some of them practically born into it. The kids mourn Juntara with deep, aching sobs and long, vacant silences, but they continue. *Why can't I?*

For weeks, sleep visits me but never stays.

I was supposed to help.

I thought I could help.

They were the best doctors in the world.

She was laughing. She was cooking. She was happy.

The thoughts are endless. Senseless. All I want to do is talk to her one more time. I decide to write her a letter.

Dear Juntara,

It was just a week ago that Kate and I packed up our backpacks and left for your village. Kate brought your school backpack from London, filled with all the gifts you chose for your family. I packed our clothes, a jar of peanut butter, my laptop, and one bright yellow photo album inscribed with the words "sweet memories" and pictures of you, my dear darling girl.

You wouldn't have liked the bus ride. Those big, red double-decker buses in London spoiled us for sure. I almost forgot what a Nepali bus ride was like until I was sitting on it—jam-packed with people, animals, interesting odors, mostly broken seats, lots of dust, and not an inch of paved roads. I think our butts were jumping off the seats more than they were actually sitting on them. (We are definitely more of the red-double-decker-comfy-cushioned-seat type of gals, aren't we, J? What can I say?)

It was actually somewhat of a relief when the road ended, and we had to get out and walk—a relief until the end of the second day of walking, when our legs felt like rubber, and we got to the base of Mount . . . (you know exactly which mountain I'm talking about), and it looked like we were about to climb Mount Everest. You should have seen the look on Kate's face when I told her that yes, that was the one we had to climb. Priceless!

Everywhere we stopped, each little hut and home, village people asked about you. They all remembered you, Juntara—how you had walked that same path just a few months before on your father's back wrapped in a shawl, singing the sweetest songs. You sure knew how to make impressions on people, didn't you? Even after just a moment in passing, people remembered you and thought of you while you were gone.

When Kate and I finally made it up the top of the last big mountain, the wind was blowing and the sun was shining. We looked down into a big, green valley with patches of snow and a small, fresh spring running down the side, and we started hiking down, down, down—stone by stone, step by step—and it was beautiful and all worthwhile. I got off on the wrong track and hit a huge slope of mud. I started sliding, and before I knew it, I was on my butt, covered in mud with nowhere to go. I'd get up and start sliding again and falling again, and get up and start sliding again. Kate just about peed her pants laughing, and Daju kept yelling about my computer.

We stayed in a tiny mud hut on the side of a mountain with a little old lady who Kate said reminded her of a witch. The woman gave us a piece of plastic tarp to sleep on, and our bodies were so sore we didn't know whether to laugh or cry, so we just huddled close together by the remnants of a fire to keep warm. I'm pretty sure the last thing Kate said to me before I fell asleep was, "I think there are lice climbing all over my body."

We woke up at dawn the next morning and kept going down and down and down some more until finally, we came to your Oda. We sat on a rock, and I pointed out your house to Kate, noting the fresh grass roof that your brother and dad had put on a few weeks ago while awaiting your arrival.

Your mom and dad were sitting inside by the fire, just the two of them, and when they saw us, they started to cry, and so did we, because we miss you so much, and it's so hard and so painful not having you here. There were no words, just tears and sobs, and cries out to God.

When things were quiet, we took out your pictures, and your mother flipped through each one, putting her fingers on your face, and she said the same thing we all did: "You were just so happy—you were so happy in every picture." Much of your family had gone to plant corn, but we waited until the evening to meet them.

We walked up to your school and around your village, and we retold your story to the hundreds of people. The evening before we left, your whole family arrived, even your big didi all the way from Katampur with Rahdika. We talked and told stories and watched hours of your videos and listened to your songs. Everyone loved the necklaces you made for them, each one different and unique and perfect. Everyone was amazed by your English, and I translated what you were saying into Nepali. "I love my mother and my father, and my sisters and brother. I love my family." They heard you say this again and again, and they know how much you loved them, Juntara. And they know that you knew they loved you, because you said that too. We set up a movie theater outside with my little Apple laptop propped up on an upside-down straw basket, and your whole village watched you sing under the moon and stars. Not a dog barked and not a baby cried, and all we could hear were your songs and your words, and everyone listened with tears streaming down their faces.

In the morning, we ate fresh fish and your favorite beans, fresh greens, black tortilla, potatoes, and red rice . . . all your favorite foods that you'd always talk about missing so much,

*harvested by your family. You were right about the water in
Kalikot—it does taste fresher and cleaner and cooler. I noticed
the taste of the water this time, and I love that water too.*

*We left that morning, and it was sad because part of me
felt like it had to be the end of your story. But then I laughed
at how silly I was being, because you're here, and you were
there every step of the way. I feel your presence in every step.
I can still hear your giggles, and Kate and I both swear that
we wake up to you sleeping in between us every night. Your
story is far from over, sweet little J.*

I close my laptop and fall into deep, peaceful sleep. All she wanted
was to be loved, to come home after her great adventure, to love.
The love is with her, wherever she is.

———

IN SPRING, I get an email from an organization called DoSomething. I'd gone on a grant application tear after looking at our
bank statements and trying to figure out how to keep Kopila Valley
afloat, with over fifty kids in school and twenty-four under our
roof.

Congratulations, Maggie! You've been selected as a finalist
for our $100,000 prize.

I forgot I'd even submitted it. I look out the windows at the kind,
green mountains and wonder what I would do with $100,000.
A friendly breeze blows in at me through the window. Without
knowing it, I start singing one of Juntara's sad mountain songs,
and I know exactly what I would do with the money: the Kopila
Valley Primary School, in honor and remembrance of Juntara.

6

KITES IN THE SKY

Dear A,
I love when you're silly. I love when you keel over laughing
and have to gasp for breath. I hope I get to watch you
laugh like that forever.

—M

"*Rato!*" (RED)
   "*Nilo!*" (Blue)
"*Seto!*" (White)
"*Pehlo!*" (Yellow)

Sabita plops onto my lap and stabs a fat toddler finger toward the sky. She's barely four, but she's got the voice of a sixty-year-old lounge singer, throaty and full of warmth. I could listen to it all day long. Her sweet-and-sour kid smells drift into me, and together, in a mother-daughter heap, we watch the technicolor kites slicing and swooping above us.

At dusk in late summer 2009, right before the sun throws out its final orange punch, every rooftop in Surkhet fills with kids and their kites. It isn't some jaunty Mary Poppins ordeal. These children yell and cuss, one flyer trying to send another on a perilous dive to the ground.

"Left! Right! Higher! Get Himal! Cut Himal! Go! Go!"

Himal is the neighborhood bully. I can't help but root against him. He steals soccer balls and pushes kids off bikes.

The boys' voices crack as they watch Bhatka, who might be the best seven-year-old kite flyer on earth, send their nemesis straight to the dirt.

"Look! Maggie Mom, did you see mine?" Anjali's purple kite is performing an elegant figure-eight routine a few feet away from the testosterone.

I close my eyes and try to preserve all of it: giggles just starting to deepen to laughter, elbows and knees lost inside of doughy toddler bodies, the way they say "Mom" and want me to see everything, absolutely everything, that they do. The children have recently had their own family meeting where they decided to start calling me "Mom" or "Maggie Mom," and it feels as true to me as my own name. Sabita's head finds the most perfect spot under my chin, and I listen to her gab about the kites. It feels like the most important information in the world.

We are a family of twenty-six now, fifteen girls and eleven boys. Plus, we have four aunties and three uncles who keep things going around here and rescue us all from my cooking. We used to live in a house of six-, seven-, and eight-year-olds, and suddenly, many of them are now eight, nine, and ten. They love drawing and playing games, listening to music, hanging out, and talking with each other. The older ones are starting to care more about how they look, dress, and perform in school. They have friends who stop by to work on school projects and practice dance routines outside under the papaya tree. These days, they have ideas and opinions on bigger things than the sweetness of mangoes versus kafal berries. They've read all the Harry Potter books. They're starting to understand the world that they live in. Even with the bedbugs, occasional deworming, and frequent delousing, we are all growing well on our dusty patch of land.

We have a routine. On Saturdays, the only day off in Nepal, we head down to the silvery lake at Bulebule to bathe and wash our clothes. Dipping a foot into the still water is like breaking a mirror, and the kids love watching their reflections shatter into watery fragments. Ubji, Guianu, or one of the other aunties come with me and shampoo the littlest ones while I get started scrubbing bite-sized jean shorts and striped shirts on the rocks. It takes forever. I normally start to dream about an industrial-strength washing machine with a drum the size of a smart car when I'm less than halfway through, but I'm not sure I could trade the satisfaction of scouring a mud stain with a brick or the smell of clothing drying on broom grass.

During the week, things are less idyllic. The grown-ups wake early to fill our bodies with chai and brace for the clipping of five hundred and twenty fingernails, the brushing of an ever-changing number of teeth, and the endless negotiation between twenty-six bright-eyed, bare-bottomed kids and their school uniforms.

Krishna is still wetting the bed. Hari keeps hiding outside in a tree and vanishing from my sight. Goma pierces Krishna's ears with a random safety pin. Madan and Pankha get overly curious about every single clock, radio, flashlight, and blender in the house and try to take them apart. Daju grunts about kids who once didn't have electricity constantly leaving the fans and lights on and yet another bar of soap jammed into the clogged drain. Most days, we manage to get everybody to school and keep them away from the hospital. At home, nothing is perfect, but everything is right.

When the kids are in class, I wobble around the valley on my plucky scooter, looking for land to build our very own school. We won $100,000 from DoSomething and received another $20,000 from Cosmo Girl of the Year. (Nobody is more surprised about this than me.) We almost have enough capital to make it happen.

Lately, our donations have been generous and steady, aided, I'm sure, by the fact that the DoSomething folks put my face on several million bags of Cool Ranch Doritos, and *Cosmo Girl* gave me four full pages of their publication to talk about Kopila Valley as long as I agreed to undergo a makeover where they dyed my hair blond and dolled me up with fake eyelashes and share the before and after pictures. The publicity is enormously helpful, but I'm deeply protective of the world we've made for ourselves in the valley, and it makes me nervous how little control we have over the narrative once I decide to share it. My children's stories are the important ones to tell, but they're not mine to share. The same is true for a lot of our aunties and uncles. We leverage the press the best we can, but the balance between elevating voices and exploiting them is tricky. I'm happy to be eight thousand miles and a half-decent internet connection away from any notoriety whatsoever.

I spend most of autumn bushwhacking my way in and out of the jungle, tiptoeing through rice paddies, and stepping in steaming piles of buffalo dung. Just when I think I've found the right spot, I'll see a group of villagers walking down the road, yoked with buckets, and find out there's no running water, the elevation is too high for a well, there's no bridge to cross the river, or the owner is far away and hasn't been seen for years. There are acres and acres of gorgeous land around Surkhet, but this is undeveloped country. We need basic infrastructure. We can't expect kids to go to a school if there's no road that leads there.

Large property purchases are also complicated here. Land is divided up into tiny parcels among villagers, families, and neighbors—sometimes more than a dozen of them. To buy a lot, we need to find the owners and then convince them to agree on a sale price. One deal falls through, then another. I putter back home in the afternoons, defeated but still dreaming of the perfect spot with a Moringa tree strong enough to hang our swing, a nearby temple where we can put our favorite picture of Juntara, and a gurgling spring filled with the cool water that she loved so much.

In the evenings, the kids finish their chores: feeding Rumi and Beatrice, our long-suffering goats, picking up their marbles (which are everywhere), and washing our giant gong-like pots and pans. We eat dal bhat for dinner, simmered lentils as rich as bone marrow ladled over fluffy rice, and then we gather in the living room for *satsung*. *Satsung* translates (quite roughly) as "the company of true people." It can be a time for grief, gratitude, joy, or singing "The Green Grass Grows All Around" until our lungs burn. Sometimes we can cover all of them in an hour. After the sky falls dark and the night birds start screaming, after I've returned a giggling Hari to bed for the third time and the house fills with the soft purr of sleeping children, the dream of our school often takes over again:

stability growth flowers safety comfort health healing sustainability home earth love animals community green gazebos solar dance theater games play laughter goodness technology family good books vegetables nutrition fruit garden beauty cuddles trees warmth nature color cleanliness long walks field trips sanctity education empowerment co-op culture art singing human values temples crops fertile

soil traditions mindful hands bedtime stories cooking open
space stream fish prayer stars dreams wishes music leaders
kindness patience peace

I want all of it. Surkhet deserves all of it. I'll wait as long as I
have to.

––––––––

IN SEPTEMBER, ANJALI comes home from school with a pink,
swollen cheek. Her eyes, normally wild and flickering, look dead
and bloated. She's a quiet, shrunken version of herself. I wait for
the other kids to mill in through the front gates and run off to
their respective fascinations. Nisha finds a thick book. Bhakta and
Krishna attempt to do chin-ups from the bough of our tree. Ganga
puts Maya's hair in sloppy pigtails. The others scatter. Ubji Auntie
follows them, shaking her head and smiling.

I reach for Anjali's hand, and her whole body stiffens.

"What happened to your face?" I ask.

A tremor crawls across her bottom lip.

"I got a math problem wrong today," she says, sniffling. "The
teacher hit me very hard."

She points to the spot on her cheek. The tender flesh has risen
up into a mound with finger-shaped ridges. I hold her for a long
time, until her tears dry to salt. Until I know I'm able to speak
without crying myself. She's only eight years old.

Schools are different here. Corporal punishment is standard.
Teachers pace up and down the rows of desks with switches, laying
them across the back of any student, even the very youngest, who
misbehaves or underperforms or forgets their tie. If the teacher
needs to step out of the room, the class captain, the top student
in class, takes over the duty, walking up and down and beating his

or her classmates. It's abhorrent but completely accepted. I bring up studies with the principal, showing the damage that physical abuse can do to the learning environment. I plead with the school and teacher to try another way, but to them the idea seems, at best, absurd. I'm a guest in this country. I try my best to respect the culture, but the beatings are too much.

In the month that follows, Nisha is smacked for wearing her sandals to school while her shoes were being fixed at the cobbler, and the boys who get class captain cry because they don't want to hit their friends. Hansaraj becomes cripplingly shy. Rupa is frustrated, as any eleven-year-old kindergartner would be. Little Maya has behavioral issues and curses like a sailor whenever she's upset. The street kids and rock breakers in our scholarship program struggle just to get to class and often have to choose between their next meal and their next class. The teachers already seem to have given up on them. One of the girls from the bus park stops going completely, and when I track her down to find out why, she holds up a shred of her school tie and tells me that rats ate her uniform. I look down at her arms, covered in welts and small purple bruises. Her clothing isn't the only thing the rats have been gnawing on. School should be a safe place, but instead our students are more afraid of their teachers than they are of contracting rabies. The day one of our eight-year-olds doesn't show up because her uncle lit her backpack on fire in a drunken rage, I'm so desperate to build our school that I almost start digging a foundation in the front yard.

"Our school will be different," Tope promises me on the phone. "Be patient. These things take time. In Surkhet, they take a very long time."

Tope and Kusum are moving to Surkhet. It was always part of the plan. Tope will be coming on as a full-time, on-site director of operations, and I need him here now more than ever. Tope loves Nepal, and he knows it in a way that I don't and never will. We're good partners and near total opposites. When I'm furious and emotional and yelling at some government official in broken Nepali, he's gentle, clear, and pragmatic. When I want to wring a teacher's neck, he appeals to their heart instead. I learn to temper my fiery frustration and impatience and sit back and watch him and the rest of the team. Tope is an orphan, just like our Kopila kids. He built a life for himself and his family after losing absolutely everything. There is no better example of success for them to see every day. There is no better example for *me* to see every day. Tope is why this work matters.

"Don't worry, Maggie—you just work on finding the land. I'll talk to the school. You guys enjoy the holiday," he reasons.

Dashain is the largest Nepali festival of the year, and school is out for an entire month. It comes in a burst of color, sweet smells, and music, and Surkhet becomes a dancing goddess for a full thirty days that culminate in yet another festival, called Tihar, the festival of light. Men cover their homes in twinkling bulbs and luminaries, and women make beautiful *rangoli* with brilliant colored powder and crushed rice on the ground in front of their doorsteps. They look like the mandalas from one of those adult coloring books people do on airplanes to relax. In this city, where everybody works their bodies lean, holidays are a time for resting, feasting, and worshipping.

But I spend most of Dashain wondering what schools really are here and what they should be, what childhood is and what it can be. I find magazine cutouts and stick them on a piece of cardboard over my desk.

KITES IN THE SKY

On the first day of Dashain, we wake up at five in the morning and bathe in the spring. The stars are still out, and the children are quietly excited. Some of them are half-asleep and shudder as the water hits their backs. Others are so riled up about eating fried dough and fresh vegetables from Devi Auntie's garden that they hardly seem to notice the goose bumps forming on their arms. Bhakta and Krishna are wary of the whole thing. They only begin to relax when I confirm that we're not going to kill Beatrice and Rumi, as custom normally dictates. Dashain is a terrible time to be a goat in Nepal. We can give the gods some fruit instead.

We walk together, the whole sprawling family, to Dhoti Bhajey, the little brick-colored temple up the road from Kopila Valley. The breeze delivers scents of mango and incense and butchered animal straight to our noses. Sabita and Sundar try their best to look somber, with red tikka on their foreheads and sacred grass behind their ears, but before long, they're playing like a pair of river otters. Neighbor after neighbor stops to smile and watch them bat at each other, and I wonder how a culture and a world that so celebrates children can also fail at protecting them.

It isn't simple, I know. How can we alleviate suffering and improve the lives of children without westernizing the world? How do we create a school that preserves Nepali tradition but rejects hierarchy? What should *my* role be? Does knowing something different mean that I know something better? It's not like America has any of this stuff figured out.

Anjali and Nisha take turns carrying our offering: homegrown papaya, furry pink lychees, coconut, and green bananas. Maya sticks a hunk of coconut in her cheek, and I pretend not to see.

One by one, we each carry our fruit up the steps of the temple.

I have to do something. They need a safe place to learn.

That day, I ask for clarity.

———

NOVEMBER COMES AT us like a thief, stripping our gangly tree of everything but the bark and sucking the heat from the air. I've stopped pining for my dream property and have started thinking more intentionally about what it is that our children actually need from an education. I don't know if it's the computer lab and the Future Business Leaders of America club I had. I begin to worry less about what they need to learn and more about what I need to learn.

One afternoon, Ubji Auntie, Daju, the kids, and I are frantically cleaning out the vegetable beds and laying compost for a winter crop: pumpkin, bitter greens, and cauliflower. Ubji stops tilling the soil and begins cutting potatoes into a bowl.

"Oh, we're having potatoes for lunch?" I ask.

"No, we're planting those," Daju says, pointing at the garden.

"What do you mean? You're cutting potatoes to *plant* them?"

Everybody stops. The kids' faces scrunch up, and their heads cock to the side as if to say, "Is this really the woman who is raising us?"

Then they begin to howl.

Ubji smiles. "Maggie, how did you think we get potatoes? You have to plant a potato to get a potato! What? Did you think they had seeds?"

"No, I guess I just never thought about it." I shrug.

"You don't have potatoes in America?" Ubji asks.

"We do. I just never planted one." I haven't put any thought into how potatoes become potatoes. Our kids have been growing food for as long as they can remember. Together, we toss the slices into the dirt and cover them.

There are countless other moments like this. I call a bull a cow in front of a group of villagers, and they laugh so hard you'd think I confused it with a river dolphin. I find out cows need to have a baby before they can give milk, that they're not just born glorious piebald milking machines. And then! They have to get pregnant again and again! I try to buy a goat and get slammed by the uncles for getting cheated. "She's an old grandma!" *Bhaje*— "grandma"—they name my sweet old lady goat and laugh. I'm not just agriculturally inept either. The four-year-olds are better at meditating than I am, and the six-year-olds are better at sewing. All these years, and my rotis are still malformed. Sure, I can write you an essay, but I can't feed, clothe, or soothe myself. The gaps in my own education are significant, especially in Nepal. I studied biology and debate, but what good is learning to argue with people when you don't know how to care for them? I see how well the kids learn from the aunties and uncles and realize that I might not be their best teacher.

My vision for the school begins to shift. I picture a dedicated Nepali teaching staff, a well-rounded education in and out of the classroom, and a deep respect for both tradition and modernity.

As a team and a board, we start sketching up the concept of a full-service community school that serves the students like ours who need more services, including school meals, after-school support, counseling, home visits and family integration, special education and remedial learning. This would also give us the opportunity to step outside of the standard rote-based memory and by-the-textbook learning style, and into more of the life skills, cultural and ancient knowledge, and place-based and experiential learning we wanted to integrate. We could bring on experienced social workers and a health and wellness team to make sure that the child and the community are both uplifted. We've started to naturally build a team of people who have similar ideas and beliefs, who love kids and have the skills and experience to make a community school vision into a reality.

When Tope and Kusum arrive in Nepal, we stop looking at properties and take a seven-year lease on a big plot of rice and farming paddy across the street from our home. Starting small and one step at a time, we build our schoolhouse from bamboo stalks and plywood, letting love guide us at every turn, which is the best and only way to honor Juntara and our future students.

The doors of the Kopila Valley School open in 2010, and right next to it, we begin construction on a small health clinic to make sure that all of our students are healthy enough to learn. It isn't the sprawling green campus of my dreams—I know we'll get there one day. It's made of sticks and the grounds are muddy, but it's a place where children can access education, safety, food, clean water, and, most importantly, love. For two years, we work and we stumble and we try our best. It is not perfect, but it is right.

7

SISTERS

Dear K,
You ask questions endlessly and on repeat, "What's this?
What's that? Where did she go? Why, though?" Every
single answer leads to another question.

—M

DON'T THINK NAMRAJ would have made it on the mountain. He's from Kalikot, but he's about as rugged as a lamb. He's our first baby. While the other kids are content to hose each other off in the side yard, Namraj insists on bathing in a large red bucket filled with ninety-five-degree water and tearless baby shampoo. I frequently remind him that in his village, they would just dunk him in the river and let him air dry, but it makes no impact. His mother, Pampa, my friend, passed away suddenly several months ago, and long before that had made me promise to take care of her children if anything ever happened to her. "Anything" happens frequently here.

The auditorium is hot. A Surkhet March is like a New Jersey August, the weather jumping from beautiful to hardly bearable and then back again by evening. Most days, the sky is thick with clouds, but today, the afternoon sun has stretched itself to lounge over the tin roof. All around us, Kopila Valley School (KVS) students, parents, and neighbors are melting in their long sleeves, packed together in the open-air building and waiting for our (very) hotly anticipated 2012 theatrical production to begin. The kids have chosen *Annie*.

My sister Libby and I are sitting cross-legged up front, inches away from the lip of our tiny concrete stage. Namraj is braiding his forearm into my hair and gumming my collarbone.

"Look!" Libby whispers. Two sets of feet appear under the large red sheet.

Stage manager Roshni hisses something at little Asha, whose only job is to tug on the string that opens the curtain. They bicker for a few seconds, and then with a lurch, the big swath of fabric curls into itself. Libby cheers quietly and tickles Namraj on the belly. He looks like he wants to murder her in her sleep.

"Molly," a second grader named Jarna, shoots up from her imaginary cot and lets out a piercing cry for her mother. A hand-scrawled sign that says "Municipal Girls Orphanage" in Sanskrit hangs down from the back wall behind. We take it all in, a troupe of actual orphans from Nepal playing pretend orphans from the Lower East Side. It's enthralling and mildly horrifying.

"This is cute . . . and kind of dark," Libby whispers.

I shrug at her and smile. It's nothing new. We always let the kids pick the play, and they always pick something twisted. Last year, they chose a modern-day version of Cinderella about a young girl working as a domestic servant. A few weeks ago, we were treated to a KVS original about alcoholism. Hikmat, our seventh-grade soccer star, played the role of the drunken father so believably I thought he might actually hit his children, Shova and Krishna Bogati, as they huddled in a corner.

Onstage, little Nisha breaks character to wave at us. Then the orphans link arms and launch into "It's the Hard Knock Life."

Broadway doesn't know the half of it. All we can do is sing along.

Libby has been in Surkhet for well over a year now, teaching English at the school and helping me with the kids at home. I needed her to come. I'm mom to over thirty now, toddlers to teenagers, and I'm struggling. I haven't slept in six months, and my nerves are toast. Teeth are missing from the back of my mouth. I can't seem to recover from one day before another begins. Life comes in and out of our community rhythmically, in big foaming waves. It overwhelms me and then suddenly recedes. Birthing and burying. Birthing and burying. The school opens, a village floods. One mother welcomes a baby; another dies of typhoid. We try to help; we fail. There is little time here for either celebration or grief. I put on toughness like a suit in the morning, but over time, it becomes flea bitten and corroded, like everything else. My mind and body are wisps of what they used to be.

I have more support than ever. Tope and Kusum are finally here permanently. We have capable teachers and eager long-term fellows who we bring in for expertise and long-term support. There's a nurse at the clinic and principal Jeff in the office. We have a mental health counselor visiting from the States and are onboarding a social worker and counselor. But I've never felt more alone. Everybody else here seems to move easily with the cadence of this place. I can't.

Shova suddenly sneers onto the scene as evil Miss Hannigan, strutting down the stage, nose in the air, pair of broken sunglasses on her face, and hands on her hips. The whole crowd cheers. Except for Namraj, who frowns and releases a load into his diaper so extraordinary I can feel it rumble into the world through my jeans.

"It was me," Libby whispers playfully as Namraj continues to fart.

Nothing cures loneliness like a sister.

Just a few days later, the school year ends. Children bust out of the gates in a big navy cloud of uniform, chatter, and song, excited for a whole month off to celebrate Nepali New Year and Holi, the festival of colors. We've had a good year. The kids aced their exams, and attendance improved. Meelan, whom we hired to take over health and wellness, was able to get many of the students immunizations and dental exams. We opened a counseling center, where women and children can get help if they need it, and we started to do home visits to make sure our families had the support they needed. Nothing was seamless, of course. There were fistfights and scabies outbreaks. Teachers would quit suddenly, and some kept asking if they could hit the students. Kids enrolled in school too late and, having missed critical learning periods, became demoralized and stopped coming. For our poorest kids, managing the demands of school and work was an impossible battle. It was a battle for me too. It still is. I worry about every single student, and with the political strikes and frequent rumblings of unrest, none of us are even sure if school will be able to open again for the next academic year.

The government is under pressure to draft a new constitution. After the armistice, peace was formalized, but it never really flourished. Over the holiday, Maoists arrive in our district and *bandhs* (strikes) become frequent. Participation is not optional. During a bandh, everything that's told to shut down shuts down quick, including the schools. Our most vulnerable kids, the ones who rely on us for food, clean water, and healthcare, go without.

Institutions that defy the order are punished, stoned, vandalized, or worse.

KOPILA VALLEY OPENS its doors and abruptly shuts them only one week into the new school year. The bandhs start up again. Kusum and I take turns putting Namraj to sleep. One night, he's with me when it begins. He clings to my belly and snores into my skin, sounding like a kazoo. I count the hungry mosquitos on the net while watching him sleep, desperate for sleep myself.

A rush of air, thick with dust and gasoline, busts through the open window in my apartment. A speaker crackles, and a militia-man who sounds like he's speaking through his nostrils announces tomorrow's instructions:

No driving.
No shopping.
No school.
No temple.

"Again?" Libby groans. Half-asleep, she stumbles into my room and flops facedown onto the bed, hair falling like fresh-cut wheat. For a kid from the suburbs and a Division 1 college soccer star, she's adjusted relatively quickly to political unrest at her doorstep.

Echoing our neighbor up the road, she sighs, "Don't ask when there's going to be a strike in Nepal—ask when there's *not* going to be one."

We poke our heads out onto the balcony. A few guerillas hop out of their janky brown truck and drunkenly poke at our fence with their rifles. One of them takes a piss in the driveway.

Occasionally, they shake us down for money or food but we never have any to spare.

"Are you scared?" Libby asks me.

"No." I'm not sure why I lie to her.

I'm not afraid of the Maoists. They almost seemed to *like* me in the early years, and nobody in their right mind is going to throw a Molotov cocktail into a children's home. We are doing the work and trying to create the Nepal that all of these political parties claim they will do once they come into power. Things are changing though. The bigger Kopila Valley gets, the more we seem to encroach on their ever-growing territory. They seem angrier and bolder. They aren't thrilled when we decline again and again and again to give them the money they request.

Daju, our unofficial ambassador to the various political sanctions, meets them at the gate. He tells them again, his steady voice reverberating through the neighborhood: we're not political, and all the money we have is for the children. They are welcome, like everybody else, to use our well. The men wobble around and mutter a few threats before driving off, sending another stinky gust through the window.

"It's fine," Daju calls up to us, shaking his head and heading back to his apartment.

Libby and I decide to peer in on the kids, just in case.

Nobody is awake when I pad quietly into the girls' room. Shanti stirs a bit, and Maya delivers a smile to me from the middle of a good dream. I pull her Minnie Mouse pajamas down over her belly and give it a pat. She's as chubby as a city racoon.

The ruckus has gone completely unnoticed.

They've slept through worse, I remind myself while watching their chests rise and fall like bellows.

These are children of war, many of them orphans of it. The lean, leathery men wearing ammunition belts with bullets like teeth are characters from their earliest memories. Violence is a part of the landscape. Illuminated by a web of stars out the window, I watch the children resting heavy on their backs, arms stretched wide, fearless and unflinching even in their sleep. They have lost everything. I often wonder what's left for me to protect them from. What can I give to them to possibly make up for what has been taken?

Love is the only restitution. It isn't enough, but it's everything I have.

Libby joins me, leaning against the doorjamb and watching the sisters in their beds, heads pressed together and bodies tangled together in trust and love.

"Were we ever that cute?" she asks.

"Not a chance," I answer, and we head back to bed for another few hours.

Electricity flashes on and off for the next several days, and the faucets are dry. With no gas to cook with, Bauju does her best, making roti for fifty over a fire. The kids run wild, and I'm shocked that the house survives them. Madan throws a *Pocahontas* DVD off the balcony, and Maya cuts her pants off with a pair of scissors. Krishna Bogati chases a big, fat mouse out of the kitchen, and I catch Shanti stealing. Again.

The bandh lifts by the end of the week, and classes at Kopila Valley resume. My nails have been gnawed far down below the quick, and what's left of my molars are ground flat as a cow's. The plates inside me begin to shift again, but not in a good way. I can't sleep. The baby is driving me mad. Every day, our counseling center fills up with battered women and girls, moaning, begging us for help. I worry into the night about how much longer a country fighting for its future can continue to ignore its women and girls. After way too many years of white-knuckling it, I start to lose my grip.

The days are tense and sobering. A girl wanders in barefoot one day and sits silently by the desk, swinging her feet back and forth under her plastic chair. I watch her. She's small and thin, but not frail. Her eyes are clear, and her skin is glowing. I'm relieved that she's healthy and fed.

One of our counselors, Sabitra, emerges from the office, with a pregnant woman who looks as though she'd been punched square in the eye. Her five children follow her out the door, a row of wide-eyed ducklings. Another assault case. The men who drank a little are drinking a lot now. We see the proof daily, bloodied and begging for a job or a safe place to sleep.

"Namaste." Sabitra leans down and smiles at the girl, who honestly doesn't seem troubled at all.

"Namaste, didi," she answers back politely. Then, matter-of-factly, she says, "I need twenty thousand rupees."

Sabitra softly tells her that we're very sorry, but we can't give her money. That isn't what we do here. The girl looks at her, then me, and suddenly falls to the floor in a panicky fit. She cries and flails like a goat about to be slaughtered for stew.

"Twenty thousand rupees," she sobs. "I need twenty thousand rupees."

We lift her to her feet, lead her into the office, and sit her on the rug, where she whimpers and moans. I get a glass of water and bring some leftover roti from the house, which she stares longingly at but doesn't touch. In a few minutes, she catches her breath and looks stoic again.

"What do you need twenty thousand rupees for?" I ask.

"That is how much I cost."

The girl is a domestic servant. She's thirteen years old, and her parents sold her to a rich man to pay off a debt. Even her parents won't take her back. The man she works for makes her touch him, and he touches her. It's not uncommon here, and at thirteen, only some people consider her a child.

"I know you have money. He says I can go if I pay him back," she growls at me.

We call the police, file a report, and place her in a safe house that we trust, several miles away. We help her, love her the best that we can, not knowing the cost.

The newspapers begin to write about us, salacious stories and indictments, mostly from publications that, for years, either celebrated or completely ignored Kopila Valley. They accuse me of colluding with political factions we've never heard of, exploiting the children, and being a Christian conversion organization, which is illegal in Nepal. The government launches an investigation into our work. Nobody wants anything to do with us. The man we filed the report against is a powerful government official with even more powerful friends. And he's a Maoist. Within a month, the girl is kidnapped from the shelter. We try again to get her back to safety. We have taken on high-profile case after high-profile case in the community, and many of them are extremely sensitive and complex. Sexual assault, child marriage, domestic servitude, violence against women.

The children are on edge. Manisha cries for her mother in the night, convinced she's still alive and in the hospital. I cry for my own mother too. I'm in over my head. The organization we've worked so hard to build feels like it is in shambles. I'm afraid for my life. The community that embraced us suddenly doesn't trust us. Anger seeps like sweat through the walls of our complex, past the high boundary we have to put up, under the nose of the security guard we hire. Stones arrive with a hollow thwack outside my room, accompanied by threats to kill me. We've crossed a line. We're no longer just feeding the forgotten women and children of Nepal; we're empowering them. Nobody asked us to do that.

To keep our doors open and our children safe, we negotiate with the official. He agrees to relinquish ownership of the girl and pay the family for her education. We agree to drop the case. We make a deal like everyone else, work the broken system like everyone else. I'm not afraid of the Maoists, but I am afraid of losing my children.

Maya catches me crying in the corner of the kitchen the morning we make the agreement. Sobs rise up in clouds to the ceiling and echo through the hallway, an awful mix of shame and relief. I tell her that everything will be okay, though it's a promise I know I can't make. For the first time ever, my fearless daughter looks scared, like she just realized that her childhood was for sale.

8

LITTLE WING

Dear S,
You went from being one of the little kids in this house to
a strong, competent young woman. It feels like you grew
up overnight.

—M

B Y THE MIDDLE of summer, the volunteers and fellows working
with us go back home. In this line of work, everybody seems
to go home eventually. Except me. I dream about it often now. In
the brief moments when nobody is calling for me, glued to me,
or angry at me, I lie in bed on my back under the mosquito net,
watching it dance and billow, placing my hand on my heart and
imagining that I'm far away, in a decent neighborhood with a car
that works, in a life with less responsibility, more time, with a
decent man who loves me. The friends I met during my gap year
are finished with college, getting their first jobs, and starting to get
married now. Just a memory encased in a Crate & Barrel frame
over a warm hearth. I want to be where they are, somewhere safe
with green grass and paved streets. It's a secret that eats me alive.
I'm doing the work I chose to do, living the life I chose to live,
but I was so deeply unprepared for all of it. I'm jealous of the
breeze that comes and goes, in and out of the window, invisible,

untouchable, masked by nothingness, totally its own. The more I want to disappear, the more visible I become.

In America, BlinkNow begins to grow, faster and faster and faster. Nicholas Kristof, a journalist from the *New York Times*, writes a piece on us, and a photographer comes to Nepal to take pictures for the story. She's wearing white pants and white shoes. Surkhet is slick with mud, but she's determined to get the perfect, sunlit shot of the kids and me in front of the emerald foothills. I wear my favorite kurta and pull back my hair, a wheat-colored heap, and we trudge through the soupy paddies to find the right spot while the kids do their best to resist diving belly-first into sludge. I admire the hours and hours she puts into prepping and getting the sun just right for the shoot and tell her that any picture she likes is probably fine. Stunned, she pulls her shades down to the tip of her nose.

"Oh, honey, you don't know? This is for the *cover* of the Sunday *New York Times* and the magazine!"

All at once, childhood falls away from me like a dead skin, but adulthood—and womanhood, most of all—still feels tender, raw, brand new.

The *New York Times* debut is huge. I'm no longer a child on a bag of Doritos, spreading love and doing good deeds. I'm an adult running a successful nonprofit. I'm respected and accountable, open to praise and criticism. Forbes 400 invites me to speak at their annual conference, more papers write stories, and I'm invited on a cruise for twenty- and thirty-something entrepreneurial sorts, called "Summit at Sea."

With all the publicity, BlinkNow blows up. Our wildest dreams come true overnight and knock us flat on our backs. Tope is thrilled. My parents are thrilled. I have no idea what I'm doing, but I seem to be doing it well, according to most American mass media. Press requests and donations and tax documents come pounding in. We don't have HR people or publicity people. We are me, my dad, and a board I'm still nervous to speak in front of. The foundation is run out of the same kitchen it started in, sharing its space with a saltshaker and a ceramic rooster-shaped cookie jar.

My dad calls in June and asks me to come home and help. I'm relieved to do it. Libby says she'll stay with the kids and urges me to get back to the States for a refill.

In July 2012, I barrel into the normalcy of America the way I did the strangeness of Nepal six years ago. I eat frozen pizza from Whole Foods, sleep in, and soak for hours in the tub with bubble bath and light a candle that smells like it should be called "LAVENDER!!!!!!!," with all seven exclamation points. I put on fancy dresses and feel beautiful. I speak at Forbes after Bon Jovi and before Oprah. I don't raise any money as everyone expects me to, but I do feel excited about the future. I meet a handsome man named Shane, who takes me on dates and calls me his girlfriend and makes me feel loved. I feel normal for the first time in a long time. It feels good to have somebody hold my hand when *I* cross the street. In America, I can show up and disappear at the same time. There are no rocks through my window, no school applications to sort through, no lice in my hair, no Maoists (at least not in New Jersey). I feel just about everything a person could want to feel here.

But like all good fairy tales, it ends.

My parents fight with each other. Steve and Nancy, once so bound together in their pursuit of a happy, healthy family, are tied together by nothing after the family leaves. Without Kate, Libby, and me filibustering the end of their relationship, it ends quickly and bitterly. They skulk around the house, and I can tell they're getting divorced long before they find the courage to tell me. As my dad pours over stacks of receipts and work orders at the kitchen table, I can't help but see how my choice to disrupt the world order has disrupted theirs.

BlinkNow has gotten too big and too busy for us to handle on our own. Our arms are flailing, and we don't know what the hell to do. I call up Kim Wentworth, my now close friend and mentor and the woman who matched my initial investment all those years ago, has run successful businesses, and eats Cobb salads like a queen, and who always seems one step ahead of the rest of the world. We go for a walk at Jockey Hollow Park, and I pour my heart out to her, barely able to get the words out, barely treading water.

"Maggie, it sounds like it's time to move BlinkNow out of your parents' house, treat it like the real, incredible, thriving nonprofit that it is. I think I actually know just the person for you to talk to. I'm going to put you in touch with Hans Dekker," she says. "You've got this. We've got this."

I nod, mostly because it feels like the obedient thing to do. In a breeze of essential oils, she steps into an immaculate white Prius and drives away.

Hans Dekker calls first thing on a Friday morning, while I'm on the train to New York City. He's incredibly involved in New Jersey's philanthropic scene, and though I can barely even pronounce *philanthropy*, I know I want him on our side. He incubates small nonprofits and businesses and projects like mine and has a beautiful office in an old Victorian house in the heart of Morristown. He's warm, friendly, and straight to the point.

"Maggie! I've got the perfect office waiting for you right upstairs. You can move in on Monday."

I thank him profusely, at least ten times, and wait until the end of the conversation to confirm the most important detail.

"So, Mr. Dekker, it's free?"

"Yes." He laughs. "Completely! As long as you can put up with all of us."

———

I PACK UP the computer, the printer, and the buckets and piles of paperwork, hard drives, and cables, and load them into my beat-up old car. I give my dad, the world's most dedicated volunteer, a big, long hug goodbye, feeling a little like I'm divorcing him too.

"I'm proud of you," he says softly to me, my head glued to his chest the way Namraj's normally is to mine.

"Thank you for everything. I love you."

I peel my body from his and get into the car, honking as I back out of the driveway. It's the college send-off we never had.

The Community Foundation is a beautiful old mansion that overlooks an old gazebo carousel and a great, green New Jersey pasture. It's something straight from a Jane Austen novel, the most beautiful space I've ever seen. The "little wing" where BlinkNow will be feels enormous. An old oak staircase leads upstairs to the office, which has ancient hardwoods, antique furniture, and a bathroom. It has tall windows and tall ceilings, and my footsteps echo when I walk into the room. It feels like a fresh new start. I feel ready for the life I'm leading.

With an office space and coffee machine, I treat BlinkNow like the real career it is. I show up every day freshly showered, ponytailed, and ready to make things happen, walking down the staircase to the "big wing," to meet my other nonprofit colleagues, use the kitchen, and learn how to use the fancy printers. When I feel stuck, I wander down to Hans's office and ask for advice.

He listens patiently and kindly, even when I one day confess that I'm not the young nonprofit hotshot he thinks I am. I'm lost. I'm still learning. I'm ready to learn, but I don't really know where to begin.

"Your feeling this way and being able to say it is exactly why you belong here." He smiles lovingly. "You just need more help. You can't continue to do it all yourself."

He leans back in his creaky office chair and takes a long look out the window, deep into green fields.

"You know, I've been talking about you at dinner with my wife, Ruth," he says. "She's worked with nonprofits her whole career. Our girls are getting older, and I think she's ready to dig into something again. I should introduce you two. I think you'll hit it off."

I meet Ruth three days later and hire her on the spot. Her eyes sparkle. She practically glows. She's beautiful, put together, and exudes more warmth and positivity than anyone I've ever met. Our "interview" is more like me groveling, a desperate plea for help. She joins BlinkNow as our first ever operations director for the most menial salary an operations director has ever seen. She's our first official staff member. I have a partner in the United States. BlinkNow population: two.

Over the next month, Ruth puts the fallen pieces of the foundation back together. She goes through the bins and bins of paperwork and digitizes everything. She puts *me* back together, building me up, reminding me that I'm capable and competent, that I belong. She's more like a mentor than anything else, a working portrait of the woman I aspire to be, a bit of a big sister some days. She's at my side for events and speaking engagements, doing everything from prepping my outfit to packing me lunch and snacks, to sharing her lipstick before a big interview. Where I falter, she's steady. Where she prefers to sit in the back, I can speak out front. We're a match made in heaven. Tope agrees. Even Hans agrees. Ruth is a force—*we* are a force—and I embrace it.

We beef up the board before I head back to Nepal, and during the executive session, it's decided that I need to receive my first-ever salary as CEO and founder of BlinkNow: twenty thousand dollars a year. I balk at first, but the board insists. They also insist on a health insurance plan. With the sheer amount of stress and parasites guaranteed with my job, even I can agree that's a good idea. At first, I'm uncomfortable with all of it, but I'm twenty-six and broke. My teeth are falling out. I can't ask my parents for cash anymore. I listen to a TED Talk by Dan Pallotta, the godfather of giving (only I call him this), a titan in the nonprofit world. The more I dig in and learn about the nonprofit and "for-purpose" industry world, the more I see that things like "overhead" can have an unfair rap. A bit of growth capital is the most sustainable thing an organization can receive from an investment firm.

I swallow a big gulp of pride and have my first executive evaluation as a CEO. I get more coaching and mentoring and leadership training. I don't just feel like an adult—I am one. And for the first time in a long time, I can afford to see a movie at the theater and buy a new pack of underwear from Walgreens.

As a final stroke, my relationship with handsome Shane falls apart. He can tell I feel torn between two worlds, and we both know which world I belong in. It ends predictably, in a fiery blaze. I cry myself to sleep in the bedroom I've had since I was thirteen years old, mourning Shane and Maggie, Nancy and Steve, Juntara and Pampa, America and childhood, the life that would have been. I look around at the blue walls lightly kissed by the streetlamps outside, the trinkets and the nubby carpet. Suddenly it's a ruin of childhood, not a shrine to it. Soccer trophies I grew up believing were gold and are now so clearly plastic, I'm almost too embarrassed to look at now. The rough-coated teddy bear that absorbed my every tear seems unable to take another worry when I bury my head into his belly.

I thought I could find peace in the place I've always belonged, but it isn't home anymore. Home is where my kids are, where the morning sun cups their cheeks and kisses them awake, where I'm presented with baby toads and dragonfly carcasses from the side yard, where life is so hard and so precious.

I know where I belong now, even though belonging is never easy.

9

BOKSI

Dear Big K,
Whenever you can tell I'm worried, you always say, "Don't
worry—everything is going to be okay," and it's always
comforting the way you say it. No matter where you go or
what you do, I'm always here.

—M

TOPE PICKS ME up from the airport in the jeep, solemn and
sitting straight up like a cartoon of someone driving, putting
a damper on my strong, American hit of girl power.

"How was your trip?" he asks, but he doesn't seem deeply interested in how packed the flight was or what I ate on my layover.

Slowly, more slowly than normal, we drive through Surkhet.
The market is quiet and sullen. The streets have been emptied of
their sounds and spices. Men with guns lounge against the statue
that once was King Birendra but has now been knocked to the
ground. A sad nub of smashed concrete is all that's left where his
statue once was, cold, despondent without his giant armful of
children. Garbage bakes in big brown piles on the curb. There are
no women anywhere.

"What's going on?" I ask Tope.

"Maggie . . ." He takes a breath so long it appears to exhaust
him. "It's getting worse."

The bandhs have started up again. The government and the Maoists are feuding. The *Maoists* and the Maoists are feuding. The kids and aunties have only been able to leave the compound a few times—once to stand in the ration line because our food orders were late, and another couple times when school was actually allowed to open. Hardly anybody else showed up, including the teachers. The reporting center has never been busier. Tope is not a worrier, but he *is* a former refugee. As long as his memories persist, the threat of violence does too. It's a fog that sinks closer and closer to us, but always stays close to him.

"Men have been showing up at the house more often," he says. "We need to be careful. Maggie, *you* need to be careful."

In September, one of our brightest girls, Shirisha, stops coming to school. She's a star student, quick with answers, stories, and jokes, a badminton champ, best friend to Karma, Rupa, and Goma. She wants to be a nurse one day and Taylor Swift the next. She's a perfect picture of fourteen years old, obsessed with her friends and her school, just beginning to imagine her future. She was there, *so there*, a part of our community, and then she was gone.

After a few days of absence, we go to check on her, me and the big girls, driving by yellow fields and snooty cows to her village. After asking around, we find her in a mud hut with her new sister-in-law. She's been married. Coolly and robotically, she tells us all about the impressive man she's been married to. He's well respected in the village, and she loves him very much. She won't be back to school. She'll be living in her husband's home, making meals and housekeeping instead.

"I'm a wife now." She says it with more defiance than pride, more anger than love. I don't know what happened to the girl who sang songs on the stage at school and wanted to work at the hospital.

The girls plead with her to come home with us. They hug her and weep, smearing her tikka and crying into her hair. She pushes them aside.

"I want you to go," she spits at us.

"You're fourteen. You can't know what you want right now," I spit back.

Her sister-in-law watches on, half-wolf in the corner, snarling and quiet. Karma and Rupa grab at Shirisha, and she pulls away. We try to lift her, sobbing, into the car for a counseling session, but she refuses. We try everything. We say everything.

"Child marriage is illegal."

"We love you."

"We can help."

"You don't have to stay here, Shirisha. You're too young to marry. You can go to school and . . ."

She doesn't care.

Before we can finish, she turns from us and runs. I take the girls home. There's nothing we can do.

Days later, an invitation arrives at Kopila. The villagers invite me to a meeting to discuss Shirisha's marriage, and I agree.

The drive to the village is pleasant and not very far. I go alone this time, hoping to make some headway with the elders. The mustard plants are fragrant and bow down nobly to me when I pass, heavy with their seed pods and star-shaped petals. A parade of brown cows strolls up the road in front of me, hips popping and rolling like skin-covered gears. One by one, they stop to drink water from a rubber trough and veer off. As they do, I notice that the village is empty.

There isn't a soul in the fields. It doesn't make sense. The buckwheat is hairy, desperate to be hewn, and last week there were laborers everywhere. I park by a pair of amber-eyed goats, who greet me with green foam dripping from their lips to their beards.

A woman retrieves a squealing baby from the dirt. He grabs one last handful of dry earth and watches, totally romanced as it slips through his fingers. The woman looks at me for a second before ducking into a mud house. Her eyes are a warning, coffee-black and pleading. For what, I'm not sure.

Once I see them, it's too late.

"*Boksi!*" ("Witch")

"*Kukurni!*" ("Bitch")

My breath is the loudest sound on earth, and time slows to a slither. I retreat to the back of a bunker inside myself that I didn't know existed. The men close in from all directions, more of a procession than a mob. Their faces are hungry and calm, like packs of meat-eating creatures from the mountain.

Help. Help. Help.

I want to scream but I don't. I can't. The fabric at my neck tears loudly. One of the men waves the scrap of shirt joyfully, a kid with a kite. There are women there, too, in the background. I grasp for them with my eyes. Tryingly.

"*Boksini! Boksini!*" they yell. "You witch. Go home."

Bucking against the hands that grab, shaking fists and pointing fingers, my body twists. Someone starts to laugh, shrieking like a myna bird, and I hear more fabric rip, feel more of the air on my skin. I'm trying to string all the words and sentences and phrases together. About respecting their culture and not getting involved in places I shouldn't. A boy about fourteen years old, the same age as my oldest boys, cranes his neck and spits on me. His eyes flash from the thrill of it.

Somewhere in the deep of me, I knew this would happen. Maybe not today, but at some point. Nobody invited me to come here and do this work. I have questioned it hundreds of times. Maybe I should leave?

But still, there are girls breaking rocks in the river. Still, there are girls who never get to belong to themselves. Still, there are girls who believe they're invisible. I can't unsee them.

The sky shrinks into a blue strip as more wild-eyed villagers come to watch me cower. Suddenly, a pair of steady arms reach for me. I'm not sure why I trust them, but I do, maybe because they belong to a woman. I let the muscular current pull me through the pack and into a cool, dark home. The whole thing lasts less than five minutes. It seems like hours.

"You can wait here, didi. Don't worry about them," she assures me, slamming a metal gated door and shrugging like a public beating is just some silly pastime.

I shake and shake. I reach for my flip phone and call the chief of police, who at this point I have on my speed dial. The woman sings to me and covers what's left of my torn clothing with her red shawl. Her rice cooker hisses, and her children watch me quietly from the corner, like a set of matching dolls. After a few minutes, one of them shyly asks me how I got so pale.

I'm so grateful for the smile I could cry.

The crowd bores of me little by little, just as the woman promised they would. The screaming dulls to sputtering and then dies out completely. The only evidence of any trouble is a piece of fabric and a few stones. The police eventually show up to escort me home. I thank the woman and run to the police jeep as the sun begins to dip to the ground. They say the case I file for child marriage won't go anywhere because Shirisha and her relatives are all on board with the nuptials.

When Tope sees me, his face is relieved but solemn.

"I don't know how many times I have to tell you not to fight every fight. There are some fights that can't be won. You need to learn to choose your battles. Think about what you have to lose! And for what?"

He turns away and heads to his room.

In the cold shower, scrubbing off the dirt and grime and spit, the tears finally come. I realize Tope's right. This isn't the first time I've walked into a situation I shouldn't have. I've picked fights with drunks who hit their children and probably wouldn't think twice about hitting me. I've confronted abuse, neglect, and assault with the same rage and disgust that poured down on me today. Maybe I should hand things over to the police? But they don't seem to show up unless I do. Maybe I should learn to walk away? But *how*? How do you walk away from another human begging for your help and not at least try? I can choose to confront the monsters who pollute this community or live with the ghosts of their victims. I can't stand the idea of another woman silenced and sent back to a man who will beat her to death. I can't stand the idea of another little girl forced to marry her rapist. The more I try to fix it, though, the more it breaks me.

The water pours off the ends of my fingers. They're shaking. It feels like they have been for years. Every time the phone rings or I lie down to sleep or I hear a scream faint enough to be either joy or anguish, in my mind I see the shapes of a thousand bruises. My thoughts turn around and around until they become their own sickness. I can't keep going like this, but I can't seem to stop either.

As I tuck in Karma and Nisha that night, they ask about the meeting, and I tell them there was nothing I could do. In this particular instance, Shirisha wants to be married, and her family approves. They even have a new birth certificate that matches the legal wedding age. We can't force her to leave against her will. We have to let it go and hope she's okay. Their faces fall. So does my stomach.

"Thank you for trying, Mom." Karma smiles sadly.

Rupa hugs me tight, and I wonder what I could have done differently. I feel like a thin gray shadow of the warrior they think I am. I watch my children fall asleep and vow quietly to myself and to them that I will never, ever put myself in a position like that again.

The next morning, I wake up, wash my face, dress for school, and help Bauju get the little kids into their clothes.

I don't tell anyone what happened in the village, how scared I was, how stupid I was to go alone, how my voice forgot to scream when it needed to. Day after day, I remind my girls to be strong and use their voices, while my own trembles in my throat. Night after night, alone and in bed, I unravel my experience in the village, remembering the faces, the angry faces, the stones in hands, the cool weather, and the scary, foreboding quiet. For the first time, I understand the eerie hush inside our reporting center, the women and children who come in phlegmatic and detached, sheltered inside themselves. In this world of girls and wives, it is dangerous to be a woman. It can even kill you.

October 2012 brings a heavy rain when we least expect it. Chunks of the mountain slip away into the earth, burying patches of forest like treasure. The paddies flood, and the boys morph into a Nepali Mountain Dew commercial, sliding through the mud on their bellies and trying to out-scream the weather. School closes for the Dashain holiday, and when the storms finally break, we all load up to work on our new land. One day, it will be the home of the Kopila Valley Campus.

The perfect piece of land that I've dreamed of for years for our expanding school surfaces one day. Our organization purchases it, a large, sun-drunk plot overlooking the greenest corner of the valley, in May. There's a small golden temple shaded by a gang of muscular bodhi trees and a burbling stream that rushes over smooth black rock. There are meadows for our animals to graze, free from little hands and flying soccer balls, and the soil is so fertile it rebels against us each time we whack it with the sickle, growing within days into taller, denser, and more fragrant bush. Our jungle is its own green planet. The stress of the bandhs, the sorrows and the faces of the women and children can't reach us through the overstory. We're lost boys and girls, architects of wild dreams, and masters of a leafy, limitless universe. BBC says it reminds him of *Jurassic Park*. Little Bishal agrees, though he's not old enough to watch it yet. They go hunting for dinosaurs in the thicket with their homemade bows and arrows. Sabita and the little girls pretend they are fairies and fly around the fruit grove.

Here, I'm filled with hope. Here, I forget all about the bandhs, what happened to me in the village, what it is to be a woman. The newspaper stories died down after the investigations, and a look into our procedures and documentation revealed that we weren't in fact doing anything we had been falsely accused of. If anything, it helped us stay on our game to make sure we were compliant and transparent. The community seemed back on board and embraced us again, like somehow we had proven that we could take a little heat and were there to stay. Our Nepali team was expanding and with that we had more allies and community representation.

The fruit trees on our new land are luxurious, practically burdened by guava, papaya, and pink lychees. Shanti and Maya pluck fruit and berries from the flouncy branches and stash them under their shirts. The big girls—Karma, Rupa, Nisha, Anjali, and Goma—are in stitches under the boughs, talking about Justin Bieber and Akshay Kumar, who reminds me of a Bollywood Don Draper. They argue with the passion and humor that only sisters can. Goma is a Bieber girl; Karma and Nisha are team Kumar forever and ever. They're getting older. Their bodies have softened and grown curves, and they're no longer children here. The little girls they played with in their villages are married and have babies now. Soon, the weight of being a woman is something we'll carry together. I think they realize how close in age we actually are. I become less of a mother figure for them and more of a big sister.

The aunties are having a quiet and grave discussion a few feet away from me while we all collect stones for a retaining wall. They look over at the girls and frown with narrow, worried eyes, and I hope they're also having an honest conversation about the virtues of Justin Bieber's hairdo.

Tara, one of the newer caregivers, a gentle woman in her forties, touches me softly on the arm.

"Maggie Miss," she says, and takes a deep rumble of a breath, "we cannot let the girls near the trees like this."

She shakes a finger at Karma, who lets out a big belly laugh.

Tara's eyes grow as big as pies, and she lowers her voice: "You know . . . they are menstruating."

In midwestern Nepal, women and girls are considered tainted when they're on their periods, bringers of blights, diseases, and curses. There is a strict set of rules called *chhaupadi* that women are expected to follow. When menstruating, women are forbidden from household activities. They can't touch the food or water supply. They must sleep outside in barns or cowsheds. They aren't allowed to enter temples or schools, and they can't look at family members, especially men, in the eyes. Even new mothers, still bleeding from childbirth, have to sleep outside until it stops. The government outlawed chhaupadi in 2005, but it still happens all the time. The seventh- and eighth-grade girls still miss class when they bleed, and the papers still print stories about women dying of smoke inhalation asleep in their shacks. One of our very own little first graders dies in a chhaupadi hut while sleeping with her aunt. We can't get her to the hospital in time. It practically breaks me.

Nisha leans against the plum tree with a Harry Potter book, and Tara gasps, looking like she could cry from the stress of it all.

"Please, it's not right. Maggie, the gods will be angry. Bad things can happen." She begins to tremor and shake as if she's being exorcised.

"The trees will be fine, didi," I assure her. "We don't believe that here." I start to rattle off facts about the female reproductive system and modern times and the fact that there are pads and underwear to maintain hygiene. I try to explain that sometimes culture and religion and truth get muddled around and mixed up, but it's hard to break down a belief system. The aunties swear that every bad thing that happens is because of the girls breaking menstrual rules. My words offer no comfort, and Tara walks away.

These women aren't ignorant; they're illiterate. The only story of womanhood they know is one that has been told to them by a man. There's a scary shaman who shows up at the house occasionally to shake, throw rice, and "purify us all." I try to be respectful, but the older our girls become, and the more women who die during chhaupadi, the harder it is for me. The last time the shaman showed up, I broke. I walked into the staff room where the aunties were seated, just as he was about to cover them in raw hot rice, and I screamed. At all of them.

"The girls will not sleep with the goats. They will not be forbidden from cooking food in the kitchen or the well or the fruit groves. Assimilation is important to me, but so is autonomy."

For the first time in the history of living together, I lost it on the aunties.

"If you want to do your ceremonies, you are free to do them, but not on our property! You're scaring the children."

Only some of them, I think, have forgiven me.

Thunder drones slow and ominous over the mountains, and the rain starts in. Hands clutched at her chest, Anjali sings the chorus of "Baby" by Justin Bieber, and dances to the sound of her own voice. Soon, the others join in. The girls love to sing and dance, and for some reason, they all happen to be great at it. A dagger of lightning stabs the foothills, and I think again about how dangerous it is to be a woman here.

That day in the orchard sticks with me, along with the day in the village. Our crisis center stays busy through fall. Women here are suffering. Girls are absent from class. The aunties are afraid to touch me when I bleed. In November, a few of the girls go to pick up their friend from school for soccer practice and find her hanging from a beam in her little hut with the tin door.

Suicide is the leading cause of death of girls and women here. Nobody seems to know why. More distressing is that nobody seems to care. I agonize over this little girl's death all winter, wrapped up in an imaginary conversation with her, rehearsing exactly what I would have said and picturing what she would have said in return. I ask why, why a thirteen-year-old girl would hang herself, but there are answers all around me.

The women in Surkhet struggle to feed and school their children. They labor in the fields, break stones in the river, walk miles for firewood to warm their homes. They marry at fourteen and mother shortly afterward, before they even know what love is. Women spend days alone in menstrual huts. Women are beaten in villages in the middle of the day. The memory gnaws at me.

Boksi. Boksi. Boksi.

Life is hard for everyone here, but whereas men struggle, women suffer.

How do we fix it?

How do we convince the women in our community that it *can* be fixed?

By the hot flicker of the fire, when the kids are all in bed, Tope and I sit night after night, snapping kindling on our thighs and trying to figure out how to support the women in changing their futures for the better. How do we convince someone who believes she is nothing that she is capable of anything?

We can host jewelry-making classes.

We can teach women's self-defense.

We can start a nursery school.

We can hire more women.

We can open a women's center when we build the new campus in a few years.

A few years feels so far away.

Tope looks up at our home, and a funny look crosses his face. He stands up.

"Maggie, what if we build it now? What if we build it right there?"

He points to the rooftop above the kitchen. The foundation is already there. So are the pillars. We stop for a moment and listen to the fire crackle. I imagine a big, bright room where women can learn and gather and start businesses. Where they can explore their interests and invest in themselves. I have it half-built in my brain before I can respond.

"Let's do it."

Daju orders 3,500 bricks and 300 bags of sand and cement. Kusum begins spreading the word. On a bitterly cold Saturday in January, we build it together. The brothers lay brick alongside their sisters, and the neighborhood craftsmen make the tables on which their wives and daughters will work. I get to work looking for grants and potential funders. While the men in government continue to squabble with the men in the street, a revolution unfolds on our rooftop: The Kopila Valley Women's Center.

10

THE TINIEST BUD

Dear J,
I wanted to write this to remember you just as you are, in
this pure and precious state, in your newness.

—*M*

I VISIT THE WOMEN'S Center when I want to feel strong. There's nothing special about it on its own. It's just a simple, open rectangle of a room with handsome rosewood windows that our carpenters made for us. The walls are seafoam green. We painted it not knowing that the color would bounce onto our faces and make us look carsick every time we stepped into the sun. A company of burly, black sewing machines line the perimeter on tables that still smell like the forest. Thick slabs of fabric hang down from the back wall like butcher meat in luscious jammy reds and peacock greens, gilded with golden embroidery and delicate, careful stitches. It is a modest, artless space, but space is a gift that all women deserve and seldom receive, especially in Nepal.

We were worried that nobody would show up when we opened in May 2013. Imagining a different future can be dangerous here; creating it is an outright act of subversion. On the first day, over one hundred local women, ages thirty to sixty, were lined up outside the door. They came with babies on their hips and in their bellies, with disabilities and hardships. They came abused, widowed, illiterate, and impoverished. They came with hope. Wonderful, intoxicating hope that stuck to everything and everyone it touched. For many, it was all they had and all they needed.

They took literacy courses and business classes, participated in parenting workshops and a seminar on human rights. During the winter, they learned to knit and crochet, and in the spring, they learned to make their own sanitary napkins. Many had never heard of them before. I showed them how to place the pad in a pair of underwear, and they all started laughing at me. The women of Surkhet weren't exactly swimming in Fruit of the Loom briefs. We ordered a pattern for ladies' underwear the next day.

After a year of learning, the women who had never held a pen-cil or sat at a desk know the basics of reading and writing. They have bank accounts and savings plans. They are certified seam-stresses who can set up and repair their sewing machines and their looms, make school uniforms, pajamas, oven mitts, and aprons, along with all kinds of Nepali traditional clothing. They're confi-dent, proud, and entitled in the best possible way. These are not the same women who walked through our doors months ago. As they wove, they unwove. As they learned, they unlearned. And so did I.

Charity is not the answer to the problems here; pity is not the answer. Investment is. I'd always believed it, but now I see it every day.

We begin sourcing our monthly textiles from the Kopila women, and the community impact is staggering. As mothers thrive, by proxy so do their children. They earn a steady income, and they're able to feed their families. With full bellies, the chil-dren perform better in school. Better school performance means more opportunity. Health and happiness go up, and crime goes down. The local economy grows. There is still work to be done, but now, after nearly a decade of hoping we were doing good work, we know for certain that we are.

I didn't know if anything would grow here, but so much has. I have. During the early treks, heading up to villages with names I could hardly pronounce—Odanoku, Ramanakot, Chaapre, Dholagohe—just existing here felt like a test. I got sick from the elevation. Stacks and stacks of blisters piled onto my heels. I couldn't speak the language or stomach the food (adjusting to daily lentils takes a colon of steel). I felt embarrassed when the men and women I met, who seemed to sail along the path laden with baskets of tea and sugar, feet hardened to hoof, would ask why my skin was so pale, if the air and the water were different where I was from. I was an extraterrestrial. Every twenty minutes, I would collapse under the pine branches, pack still fastened, like a turtle on its back, and cry, sustained only by the echo of the last spring and the dream of the next one. A hundred times, I tried to surrender myself to the mountain, but it wouldn't have me. It insisted that I keep on, learn the world before trying to change it.

What I thought would be the death of me made me come alive. The mountain held me as I played like a child, tossing smooth kidney-shaped rocks into the gorges and streams. It healed me as I stuck my broken skin into its cool puddles. It led me into womanhood, shaky step by shaky step, under the great ceaselessness of the sky. Nepal birthed my beautiful children. Nepal made me a mother.

———

UNDER THE SUMMER sun, the first Kopila buds are blooming, unfurling into kind, inquisitive adults so beautiful I can hardly stand the sight of them. Nisha, our first child to come into the home, is first in her class and continues to awe me with her perfect report cards. The middle kids seem to shoot up by inches every

month, and their mouths are filled with empty spaces and big teeth
I hope they'll grow into. I don't have to take them to the emergency
room quite as often now (except for Madan, who is quite bad at
parkour). The littles still let me hold them, but not for long. What
they want most are all of the answers to all the questions:

"Why is the ocean blue?"

"What do bears eat for breakfast?"

"What happens when you mix purple, black, and green?"

Most recently, "How are babies made?"

Even clingy Mad King Namraj occasionally distances himself
from me to join the band of brothers and sisters.

Kopila Valley is thriving too. In April, the Dalai Lama presented us with an Unsung Hero award. I'm better at speaking now,
and I think less shaky all around. I like to spend every minute I can
speaking at schools to kids of all ages. I find that there are years
of ripple effects. Former students from New Jersey tell me that
our story had a profound impact on them. They go on to work
for nonprofits or take on causes they believe in. Instead of chas-
ing careers that will bring them money or success, they realize the
joy and satisfaction that comes from using their lives and their
privilege to make a difference.

I make occasional trips back to the US for fundraising and
events, board meetings, and the nonprofit eighteen-hour-a-day
hustle. I try to sign up for trainings and classes online to keep
honing my skills, and I find the more I dig in, the more I learn.
Fundraising is still a constant challenge for me, but time after
time, again and again, little miracles of generosity happen. Ruth
continues to build a small and humble team. We find strength in
being transparent, honest and open about the challenges we have,
where our money goes, the direct impact it makes, and the stories

of the community and the people we serve. Our programs have grown holistically and organically to uplift and meet the needs of the community, and as we run out of space for expansion and growth, we begin a capital campaign to build the school and community center of our dreams.

Families of supporters who have now become dear friends step up time and time again. Chris and Lorraine Wilson call me into their office in the city where, after sharing our drawings for the school, they put down the first big investment. My friend Karen Mulvaney calls me on a walk one day. "What do you need?" she asks. When I tell her, my voice is shaking. "We believe in you; you can do this," she says, making the biggest pledge in the history of BlinkNow. There's Nico in the Netherlands who leaves us in his will and asks for his ashes to be left around the bodhi tree after he dies. There's Jeremy and Leslie who understand when we go way over budget with all the additions we make and all of the challenges we've come across. They pledge everything we need to finish off the school. Jim Duff gives me a long talk about land prices and the market and makes a pledge to buy up more real estate across the street.

It's not just the big gifts that are transformational. It's just as meaningful when an Uber driver donates their tips from the day or a tween donates their birthday or Bar Mitzvah money. A single mom who works as a waitress in North Carolina pledges a part of her paycheck each month. Nepalis around the world, grateful for the opportunities they've been given and feeling a desire to give back to their country, take on monthly giving plans with anywhere from $5 to $100 a month. Every dollar matters.

Tope and I learn to make each rupee go as absolutely far as it can. We know our success didn't come from big aid money or development dollars. It came from real people. In turn, we make sure we pay it forward to the poorest of the poor to transform their lives. We try hard to never lose sight of that. Nepal is a country of bartering, and I always smile when Tope bargains and shakes down a vendor if he feels they are over-charging us by ten or twenty rupees. He'll go back and forth with the shop-keeper until he feels like he's gotten a fair price. When he gets back in the car with goods in hand—nothing at all, because he stubbornly refused to buy something he thought was ten rupees too expensive—I give him a look. "Maggie," he reminds me, "I used to work an entire day's labor for ten rupees a day."

The team we have is rock solid. With the aunties and uncles, our fellows (who accept fellowships in their particular area of expertise and commit to longer periods of time), the clinic and school staff, and the endlessly patient and graceful Tope, the whole joint can basically run without me. Often, it does. When I am home, most days are spent mothering, and attending meeting after meeting in the office. In the evenings, I watch the kids fly their kites, not believing how far we've all come and wondering where we'll go next. I try hard to balance it all: to be present for meals and satsung and bedtime and soccer games. We finally get an internet connection at the house, and although it's intermit-tent and the power flickers on and off, I spend late nights work-ing on emails and proposals, and jumping on and off conference calls, apologizing profusely for my spotty connection.

I find deep friendships with the fellows. They come in small groups of two or three, after a rigorous application and vetting process, are dedicated, professional, ambitious, and renowned in their field of expertise. Paired with our local Nepali team, it makes for really strong progress in developing and building our programs and our best practices. The fellows are also really fun for me to have around. They give me more of a social life, and comfort in being able to hang with people my age from cultures similar to my own. I go over to the fellows' flats for movie nights, and watch actual TV shows. I finally get caught up on pop culture and all the things I'd been missing from back home. The fellows become my rocks, working hard by my side, making me laugh, calling me out on my quirks, reminding me to leave the house and work every once in a blue moon, and shaking me out of the fog I've been in from growing up too fast.

———

I'M EATING LUNCH at my desk in June, when one of our fellows brings an orphan case for me to look at.

"She's in the waiting room. I told her we can't take in any more children." Kelly shrugs.

Our house is full. We don't even have enough room for a pet mouse (though the ones in the kitchen do just fine).

"Do you think she needs food?" I ask, stuffing a heap of dhal bhat into my mouth.

"Maybe," Kelly wonders. "She looks tired. She has a baby with her."

A thin woman walks silently into my office with an infant loosely swaddled in a rag. Before I can introduce myself, she shoves the bundle toward me.

"We're full, didi." I stop her.

"Please. His mother was killed. He's not taking milk," she whispers so quietly that I need her to say it again.

"It is a boy. His mother died."

The bundle is small as a sparrow.

"Was he born today?" I ask.

"No. Two months." She holds up her fingers in an accidental peace sign and coughs.

God. She looks sick.

I take the baby from her while she hacks away in the corner of the room. The rag over his face is caked in what I can only hope is mud, and a dry, yellowish fluid. I pull back a little petal and feel myself gasp. I've never seen someone so close to both the beginning of life and the end.

His eyes are jaundiced marbles that roll back into his skull. His body is limp and nearly weightless, nothing but skin and a mop of black hair. Sweat collects on my temples, and words fall from my mouth in a nonsensical cascade.

"Clinic . . . what is this? . . . baby . . . dying . . . dead?"

I run with the baby out into the heat and toward the clinic.

"Jagat! Jagat!"

I scream our tech's name the entire distance from my office to his. When I push open the door, he's arranging a bouquet of fresh toothbrushes. They clatter to the floor.

"It's a baby," I gasp.

He pulls a fresh sheet of paper over the exam table, and I set the body down. It hardly makes a crinkle. The bright white overhead lamps come on with a buzz. We stop to take him in.

"Oh my God," Jagat murmurs.

The baby's bones bend and shift with every breath; knobs of wrists and knees wobble like jelly. His face is a thousand years old. He has worry lines and crow's feet and penny-colored skin that sags from his cheekbones and lands in a pile of ripples at his ears.

"Look at that hair." It's a silly thing to say, but this tiny crumb of a person could be the world's next great Elvis impersonator.

Jagat smiles and touches the thick mane with his fingers.

Carefully, he drops a few beads of rehydration fluid into the little mouth. Within seconds, both of us are covered in vomit and watery green diarrhea. The baby's belly is hard and distended. We need to get him to the hospital.

In the car, I hold the cold baby against the heat of my stomach, and I thank God that my friends from home are all pregnant, going on and on about skin-to-skin and kangaroo care and attached parenting. I rub his back furiously and try to remember the rhythm of the Bee Gees song they teach you in CPR class.

He perks up for a moment, blinks his brown-black eyes, and gives me a funny look.

Have we met? He squints.

And again, he drifts out of consciousness.

There's no doctor in the ER when we arrive. In all the years I've been in Surkhet, I don't think I've ever seen a doctor here. Nobody comes to help him. Struck dumb, we just stand for a few minutes while the baby leaks diarrhea into swampy puddles on the floor.

"We have to get out of here," Jagat says, and we head to a clinic across town, where his friend works.

Jagat's friend is waiting out front. He whisks the baby off to the operating room to try to find a vein that hasn't collapsed in his foot, which is the size of a Ritz cracker. Miraculously, he inserts an IV line. We all fall to the floor to breathe for a second.

The medicine takes hold quickly, and when I pull my body up from the tile, the teensy body seems to have filled with life again. His fists shoot up from the table, and he bleats at us in a soft falsetto like a faraway lamb. He blinks slowly and peacefully, looking up at the lights and stainless-steel gadgets and faces as though he's been born all over again.

"Hi, baby," I coo at him.

For a collection of seconds, his eyes pause on mine. Pupils shifting, lips just begin to move, he sings a silent song, and I fall in love. Deep love.

His fingers wrap around the tip of my pinky, and he absorbs me the way I absorbed him, his little eyes searching deep and settling on something familiar that can't be explained. We don't connect; we collide. I'm suddenly blind to everything else in the room. I study his movements like a series of miracles and proclaim them.

His hands curl and uncurl.

"His hands!"

His eyebrows rise, stretching up onto his forehead, and fall back down.

"His eyebrows!"

He grunts from the effort of being a baby. Every door inside me opens wide. Every doubt falls away. I'm swimming in my love for him.

A couple hours later, the reports come back from the lab. He has bacterial and respiratory infections. We don't know if it's dysentery, cholera, or something entirely different, but the hospital is dirty and crowded and hot. The air is hard to breathe. After consulting with the doctor, we decide to bring him home and set up an IV in my bedroom, where I'll be able to look after him. We name him Ravi. The *v* is pronounced with a really soft *b* sound, so it's something like "Raavi" or "Robby." It's a refrain I could sing all day long.

———

OVER THE NEXT few weeks, Ravi eats and he eats and he eats. His cheeks grow rosy and plump with fat. The clouds clear from his eyes, and he's strong enough to lift his chin off the ground when I lay him on his belly, the way the baby books tell me to. Our next-door neighbor, Sukmaya, comes over a few times a day to feed him her breast milk. She bundles him up in layers of clothing and blankets, even though it's the heat of summer, and does the sweetest little Nepali mom things, like blowing on him when he coughs and slathering him in mustard oil. It makes him so slippery that his torso shoots through my hands when I lift him. We spend hours picking the lice nits out of his hair and tickling him under his perfect acorn of a chin.

"You're such a good mom," I tell her as she nurses her own daughter.

"So are you, Maggie Miss." She smiles back at me. "You are the only mother he knows."

I stick a bottle between his lips and wish I could give him even a single memory of the woman who left the world so that he could enter it. All I can do is love him. And I do, in a way I never thought I could love.

When he gets stronger and the infection clears, the kids are allowed to spend time with him. No child has been so wildly adored. The teenage boys carry him around in the baby carrier without a hint of shame and take him on guided tours of the garden and the kitchen. The girls read him passages from their creepy Goosebumps books (which he appears to love) and *Anne of Green Gables* (which does nothing for him at all). The little ones plaster the wall next to his crib with messy tricolor rainbows, straight-faced stick figures, and superheroes, and they cover him in gentle, breathy kisses. The Women's Center grads make him more traditional swag than a baby could possibly ever wear, and they fall to pieces when I bring him to visit in his box-shaped hat and gold pants. He looks like the world's flashiest gnome. I worry he'll be the end of the aunties. They argue over who gets to hold him and are constantly asking me when they'll be allowed to fatten him up with ghee and bottles of buffalo milk.

"Not yet." I smile. "In just a few months. I promise."

They think about him almost as much as I do.

Even Namraj, who refuses to share me with anyone, won't sit in my lap unless Ravi can sit in his. He says Ravi is *his* baby, but really, Ravi belongs to everyone. He becomes the center of our little family. I spend all my time caring for him, feeling guilty that the school or the clinic or BlinkNow might need me, but they don't.

———

ON AUGUST 13, Surkhet floods. The drowsy river that runs through town is an angry sea. It leaps up over the banks, collecting mud houses and goats and debris, and leaving no thing or person behind. Most of our school families squat along the river. In Surkhet, it's the only place they can afford to live.

I'm in Kathmandu with a sick Ravi when it happens. I'd been in Kathmandu with Ravi in the NICU for weeks, fighting for his life. He'd been to multiple hospitals with multiple doctors telling us they weren't sure if he was going to make it. Ravi developed a series of infections and still wasn't growing as he should be. Recovery from severe malnutrition is way more complicated than simply getting food into the baby's system. Thank goodness, a telemedicine call with an international pediatrician led me to getting Ravi to Kathmandu and admitted under NICU care. The timing couldn't be more atrocious.

Our school fellow calls and tells me that some of our students are missing. I bounce on my cot outside of the NICU, trying to come up with a solution to something that can't be fixed. Hima lives at the river, and Laxmi and dozens of other children. For many of them, it will already be too late.

I look through the glass and spot Ravi, all six pounds of him, getting chubbier and snoozing away, my miracle boy, my anchor, my perpetual reminder. *You can get through anything, anything, anything.*

The next day, I drive home through the brown slop where our town used to be, rain still falling in sheets.

When I arrive, Kopila Valley School is filled with refugees. Two hundred people are sleeping under our roof, on the stage where we did *Annie*, in the classrooms and cafeteria. The aunties and uncles have been working around the clock, cooking hundreds of pounds of rice and scouting the area for survivors. The Women's Center distributes clothes and blankets, and Jagat stays up through the night, treating wounds and setting bones. Without my leadership. Our school principal appeared on the weather channel on international news. We raised nearly $40,000 for flood victims in our community. Eileen flew in to care for Ravi so we could focus on relief efforts, supporting victims, and rebuilding our community.

Slowly and achingly, our town pulls itself up from the mud. The monsoon arrives in fall, but we manage not to let it sink us. We fortify the riverbanks with sandbags, supply the refugee camps, and watch the sky. The weather seems to calm by November, and life mostly returns to normal. We celebrate Dashain, go on camping trips, and fly our kites. Kopila Valley continues to thrive. Mostly without my leadership. A strong, Nepali-led community is all I've ever wanted for Kopila Valley, even though I know it means that someday soon my role will change.

On a cool night, in the last moments before one day turns to the next, I'm mixing a bottle of soy formula for Ravi, shaking it furiously and deliriously while he watches on, delighted. A crowd of stars peek in at us through the window, as we converse in the tender, secret language of mothers and their baby sons, and everything feels perfect. I make an easy chair from my belly and thighs and sit him on it. He pulls on the bottle and looks at me. I'm so tired and so complete.

When he's done, he finds the warmest spot on my chest, and we breathe together in the quiet. I drink in the tang of his formula breath, the bathwater still fresh on his skin, the sheer joy that tumbles out of him. As a hint of gray light decorates the edges of the valley, I forgive God or the Universe or Shiva for everything that's ever been wrong, for grief and fear and doubt, for every hard day and every injustice in my life. Ravi is everything right. He's been with us for five months, but I can't remember what it felt like in a world without him. That any of us ever didn't know and adore him seems preposterous. He belongs to us in the improbable but absolutely certain way that I belong in Nepal. At four in the morning, in this world of just two, there is nothing missing. I am his home the way Kopila is mine.

"My darling boy," I ask, combing his hair with my fingertips, "where does all this love come from?"

His gums, toothless and pink, are like ballet slippers. He smiles, and a hot string of drool rolls down his chin and onto my arm.

"What are you going to be, huh? Gandhi? A CEO? Superman?"

He sits up, draws my face into his with his sausage-y baby arms, and his fantastic lashes flutter across my nose.

Yours, he seems to answer with his clever brown eyes.

I lay him on my chest, his body falling perfectly into mine, the gentle thumps of his heart rapping right alongside my own. For a minute, it's like I have two of them. Urged on by the crickets outside, the cool wind skittering across the window, and the nine pounds of dopamine on top of me, my eyes grow heavy. Because it feels urgent, I pray:

Thank you, thank you, thank you.
Thank you for these children.
Thank you for this family.
Thank you for Surkhet.
Thank you for my baby.

I repeat it a few times. I've said so many prayers since I came here, in hospitals and temples, at births and funerals, in the middle of a mob filled with men, sunk deep into the hole that became my home. I've prayed for health and safety and strength and justice.

Thank you, thank you, thank you.

What else is there to say? The words flow through me like river water, and I let myself drift away.

With Ravi, I want for nothing in this world.

11

WHITE LIGHT

Dear R,
The only thing worse than losing you would have been to
never have loved you at all.

—M

"DIG DEEP, DOYNE!"

My thighs are blocks of tofu, a pair of nervous, shivery blobs held hostage in a spandex triathlon onesie. It looks like a baby swimsuit, and I feel like a baby. Every movement is slow and requires concentration. There are only three miles left to run, up a hill, across a grassy plateau, and down through an evergreen wood that creeps up close to the Princeton campus but is careful not to disturb it. I don't know if I can make it. All I have to sustain me is the motivational barking in my head and half an electrolyte gel called "Razz." It must know it tastes nothing like actual raspberries.

The first ever Tri for Kopila was organized by Olivia, a younger graduate from my high school who while recovering from a major surgery during her junior year made a goal for herself to run a triathlon and raise funds for BlinkNow. It's become an annual tradition, and now we have a team of nearly fifty of us who compete every summer. This is only my second triathlon. I flew through the cycling, but my ribs ached all the way from the swim. I love the water, but I'd forgotten how difficult it was to float without a giant foam noodle. There's no music to listen to and no air to breathe, and the sun is just a network of white veins on the bottom of the lake.

"Wheels! Wheels! Wheels!"

———————

RAVI AND I have spent the summer months in Mendham. He needed minor surgery, and I really needed to spend some time with our BlinkNow team in our office in the US. The days here are deliciously predictable, almost musical in tempo. I work and I mother. I sleep and I wake. We visit the grocery store, sit in the stacks at the library reading *The Runaway Bunny*, and go to the rubber mulch playground, where Ravi stuffs his chubby face through a porthole in the blue plastic tunnel and shouts, "Ba!" at anyone who passes by.

Fundraising is a struggle for me. It might be the most difficult part of the nonprofit world in general. Your mission is only as strong as your funding source. I'm not good at shaking people down, or making big hard asks like they teach in the development and nonprofit management workshops. I feel like a fish out of water at cocktail hours and fancy lunches, but I'm learning and trying hard to make it. I stress about money and meeting our budget, day after day, month after month. I wake up with my heart beating fast and cortisol coursing through my veins. The hard thing about this nonprofit world is that a new fiscal year comes and the stress starts all over again. Sometimes I'm not sure we'll make it to the next month or through the next big project. Ruth and I stay up late into the night working on proposals and pitches and presentations. It gets draining and most of the time I feel like I'm exhausted and not good enough. I'm grateful for a board that builds where my weaknesses are and try to keep surrounding myself with people who have skills and strength and experience where I lack. I hope that by being myself and staying truthful and openhearted it appeals to the right kinds of people and I'm so touched when time and time again the post office box has checks trickling in. I read each note, and feel teary eyed with each and every message, each donation and the meaning behind it.

"Leave it all out there on the field!"

I left it out there all right. About two miles back in an orange porta-potty.

The road cuts left and dips down into a cool forest. Everything is a childhood friend. The cushion of needles and decay under my feet, the beady-eyed gray squirrels riddled with anxiety, the elegant mushrooms whose names are too silly and strange to forget once you've learned them: puffball, shaggy mane, Sulphur shelf. I want to *go, go, go,* but I also want to stop, draw all of it into my chest, and remember what it was like when the world was a small place. When I was kept awake by nightmares instead of flashbacks. When courage was a game played in the yard with pillow sham capes, and only good dogs and great-grandmothers left us.

"Only one mile left. Let me see you hustle."

The dignified pines thin to broom handles. I can see the color of the sky again. A "Tri for Kopila" banner flutters up ahead. Almost there.

"Push it!"

The Kopila Valley School hosted its own race back in March—a 5K for gender equality, possibly the first 5K Surkhet had ever seen. Nobody exercises in rural Nepal; you sweat out every grain of rice you eat. The students ran and organized the event with our partner organization She's The First. Many of our students are victims of domestic violence. Some had lost their mothers and sisters to their fathers. The conversation around women's rights is tense, often silenced before it can properly begin, but the next generation is noisy.

Nearly 250 runners showed up, with reasons for running handwritten on their bibs.

I run for the women in my village.
I run for my mother, who married young and never got an education.
I run for my sister, who never went to school.
I run for girls who are trafficked.
I run for a girl who works in a hotel.

When the microphone blared "GO!" the kids set out as fast as their legs and lungs would carry them. By kilometer two, they ran out of gas. I did too. It was all we could do to put one foot in front of the other and keep going. On the side of a hill surrounded by a pack of foal-legged teenagers, a lesson I'd learned over and over, since I charged at Nepal ten years ago, repeated itself: change isn't about running from something or toward something—it's about running *for* something. You can be slow. You can be clumsy. You can make mistakes. Put one foot in front of the other. Learn. Learn more, and then more after that. One day, you'll look around and revel in the fact that you're no longer running alone. You might even realize that you're no longer out in front, and you can revel in that too. Nepal is beginning to change. Not from the outside, but from within.

"Go! Go! Go!"

Back at the New Jersey State Triathlon, I cross through the finish and head straight to Ravi's open arms. Everything hurts for

days after, but we raise over $12,500 to send members of our first
KVS graduating class on to higher education. Mendham has been
good to us, but it's time to go home.

———————

KOPILA VALLEY APPEARS as Odanoku does, a pearl set gently
upon a tuft of green, protected by a golden tube of sunlight. It's
just before Dashain. The front yard is quiet when we get in. The
littles wave down at us from the roof but don't step away from
their kite strings; the middles slowly set down their books and soccer balls to give us hugs and tickle Ravi's bare toes. After twenty-
nine hours of travel, he's a delirious bucket of giggles.

The teenagers have jobs now and won't get home until the
workday is done. The boys are table bussers and baristas. The
girls teach at day cares and assist at our Women's Center. Bhatka
is shadowing a stonemason building the wall at our new campus.
Karma and a few of the others are working with local NGOs,
mentoring at-risk youth. Every day, they get a glimpse of the children that they used to be. Every day, those children get a glimpse
of what they can be. We insisted on the jobs. Daju wanted them to
learn about money management, and Tope wanted them to learn
some new social skills. I just wanted a few less than fifty bodies in
the house over the break.

One by one, late in the afternoon and into the night, they file
into the house with tender feet, rainbow-colored wads of cash,
and stories to tell me. They go on about confused tourists and
cranky kitchen staff, babies with diaper rash and kids with chips
on their shoulders. I heat up bowl after bowl of tepid goat stew
and watch them, listen to them, marvel over them. In the blink
of an eye, my children have gone from needing a better world to
creating it on their own. Bishal wants to be an engineer, Nisha

wants to be an oncologist, Anjali wants to be a writer, and Naveen Tiwari doesn't know what he wants to do, but I don't think it's working in a kitchen.

"They're like a bunch of *pirates*," he says of the line cooks, shaking his head.

Eventually, they go off to sleep or study or talk, leaving tender kisses on my forehead just like the ones I used to give to them. I sit alone in the kitchen for a while, long after my eyes adjust to the dark, and I can pick out the shapes of the pots and pans, the crevices and little splinters on the wall, the sounds of the skittering mice. The children are growing up. Next it will be Bishal, then Maya, then Namraj. One day, Ravi. I picture him across from me in a dim cone of moonlight, sixteen years old, eating leftover goat and complaining about his boss. His body will stretch out and grow strong; his scratchy peep of a voice will deepen. He'll wear a wristwatch and a button-up shirt and disagree with me.

A lump climbs up to the middle of my throat. I love and hate time in equal measure. Motherhood is forever, but childhood is just a few years. My joints ache when I rise, and I remember that time is happening to me too.

———

AUTUMN 2015 IS a fairy tale. In the mornings, a thick, downy blanket of cloud falls down from the highest mountain peaks and settles on Surkhet, lifting by noon to reveal the banyan trees and emerald paddies, full and ready for harvest. Sunshine slices through the mist and seems to cover the city in the white, protective light I've been praying for. For the past two years, autumn has brought flooding to our valley. There hasn't been any rain yet, but floods are shifty. The sky seems too beautiful to trust.

"Everything is fine, Maggie. If the rain comes, we're ready," Tope assures me.

I walk to the river with Ravi one day to check the area and make sure our families are prepared. He hangs on the front of me, heavy as hell in his carrier, limbs splayed out like a chubby sea star. I stick a hand under his butt. It's been a long time since I've walked through the city without a pressing errand to blind me from the sights and sounds. The streets are less ragged now. Smooth patches of blacktop stretch out over the places where potholes and chasms used to be. Motorbikes and cars, twice as many as I've seen before, bleep their circus horns and whir around from place to place. Women laugh together in the park, drinking chai and watching their toddlers climb all over King Birendra, who is freshly polished and handsome as ever.

"Truck!" Ravi squeals.

He reaches his hand out toward a fleet of yellow bulldozers churning up big slabs of pavement where a hotel will go. Surkhet is growing up too.

The river seems almost lonely when we get there. Only a few mud homes hang perilously over the lip of the bank, and the sound of city bustle drowns out the sounds of the women and their mallets.

"Namaste," I say as Ravi and I smile at a beautiful woman and her daughter, who is about five. We volley small talk back and forth for a bit, discussing her kids and mine, and then I launch into my friendly (but dire) warning.

"You remember the flood last year?"

"Yes, didi, we were here," she replies.

"Do you need anything to prepare? Just in case?"

"No, didi—we are ready."

And they are.

Nearly everyone I talk to has a place they can stay, with family or neighbors. They have sandbags and emergency food rations. They know where we are if they need our help. But not everyone does. The city doesn't seem to need white light. It seems to have enough light all on its own. I turn around and head home.

I begin to wonder where I fit here. There is still much work to be done, but with a rising generation of educated, enterprising Nepali adults, I'm not the right person to be doing it. I will show up for this country, these people, and their children until the day I die, but the valley is thriving. Nepal is showing up for Nepal: When school starts up again, and our tenth- and eleventh-grade students board a bus and set off to a rural area called Dhulikhel, Kavreplanchowk, to provide relief to families affected by a string of devastating earthquakes. When we take on a complex medical case, a baby called Aruna from the mountains, it isn't America or an NGO that answers our call for help—it's Nepal. Nepal connects us with senior doctors, social workers, and medical staff. Nepal sends money and brings blankets, clothing, formula, and diapers to the baby's mother at the hospital.

My dream was an empty riverbed, an empowered nation, educated children, and a promising future. It's all coming true. My heart bathes in the joy of it and drowns in the truth of it. If Nepal is showing up more, I should be showing up less. I start to wonder about a new dream.

———

ON NOVEMBER 18, 2015, we win CNN Hero of the Year. Anderson Cooper says *my* name, but the award belongs to a long line of people before it could ever belong to me. It belongs to Tope, to

Daju and Bauju, to Ganesh, who drives the school bus, and Jagat, in the clinic. It belongs to the teachers and aunties and uncles. It belongs to Surkhet, our glorious green wonder of a valley. Before all other people, our children are heroes.

The room, a room so big it could be a stadium, fills with applause and whistles that echo on and on. I stand up from my round wedding-reception-style table, with my springy hair and very nice dress, legs clean-shaven and feeling chilly for the first time in months, and I look up. Illuminated on the screen above the stage is a picture of Ravi, my reason, the love of my life, glowing about two stories tall. The rest of the room fades away, and all I see is my boy. I walk toward him. It has nothing to do with an award, nothing to do with recognition, and everything to do with how much I love him and our family. Every step toward him in my silly-tall shoes feels like a step toward peace and wholeness. I feel closer to who I was born to be and everything I've ever wanted. When I arrive at the podium, I can hardly speak. I look to Tope in the front row, teary-eyed, beaming, standing, clapping proudly, and nudging me to go ahead and speak.

I start by acknowledging Tope, who I wish in that moment more than anything was up there on the stage with me. "To Nepal, thank you so much for loving me and accepting me as a daughter, welcoming me into your country. To all of you in this room and to all of you who are watching, please, please remember that we have the power to create the world that we want to live in, just as we want it. And that's what all the Heroes here have done tonight."

I look up at my Ravi, and I feel the roots of a new dream settle inside me: *love.*

I GET BACK to the hotel, wobbly from the champagne and my beautiful, terrible shoes. I turn the shower on hot. White clouds crawl out from the crack under the door and swirl into misty tendrils. The mist weaves through my fingers and curls around my wrists, just like fog on Maha Bua. I'm reminded of home in the best and worst ways. When you reach the top of one mountain, the search begins for the next.

What will my next mountain be?

Overcome with both the joy and grief of accomplishment, I peel the clothes away from my body and step into the shower, water hitting my back with a hollow patter and leaving red spots on my arms.

Is the water different where you're from?

Yes. It is different.

I fall into the pillows and make space for a new dream.

love support Nepali local sustainable school empowerment
humility kindness mothering fearlessness
Ravi

My Ravi. The beautiful eyes that turn into little banana shapes with every smile, the teensy quartet of teeth just barely popped through the pink of his gums, the laugh, wild and ridiculous, straight from his belly. The dream is simple.

IT'S DECEMBER 30. I'm back in our bustling home in Surkhet, visiting with a friend and picking Christmas toys up off the floor: a half-dozen wooden trains, a doll who has lost all her clothing, and a stuffed dog with a soft red tongue. Anjali starts screaming.

It's a sound I've never heard before—part siren, part animal, part monster. Then others start in, crying, braying. I look out the window. The yard is completely still. The kids are chess pieces, frozen in place, needing to be plucked up and shifted. One by one, I watch them fall to their knees.

In the time it takes me to get to my feet, the house fills with mournful sobs, a dirge, the music of the undone. The stairs are nothing. I fly over them. The door is nothing. I don't even know that I push it.

The air is cold, and the ground is tough leather. Little arms lift and little fingers point, but words for all of us are impossible. The front gate is open, swinging leisurely back and forth. Just beyond it, Karma is on her knees next to the septic pit and its enormous brown puddle. Her arms are locked at the elbow, and she's pumping the heels of her hands onto a tiny chest. She stops and looks to me, eyes wide and shattered like glass.

Ravi.

His hair is a navy-colored halo around his face, which is perfect and full of life even in death. His favorite shirt with candy-red stripes is soaking wet and stuck to his belly.

"*Ravi!* My baby! My baby! My baby!"

I fall to my knees beside him in the murky wetness and throw a CPR mask that I don't even remember grabbing over his face and *pump pump pump. Pump pump pump pump.*

The harder I work to bring him back, the further he drifts from me. I can't look at him. I squeeze the bag in my hands over and over and scream like an animal.

He must have gasped for breath. He must have looked for me to save him at the surface of the water, just like that time I let him fall in the swimming pool, to teach him to fear water. I read it in my parenting book. You let them fall in once, so they're convinced not to do it again. I should have taken him to swimming lessons. I should have made sure the worker closed the gate. I should have tested the strength of the cover. I should have never let him out of my sight. Why wasn't I watching him? Why wasn't I holding his body close to mine, the way I always, always long to do? I should have been holding my baby. I should be holding him now. There is nothing left of him to hold.

I cradle him, the husk of my baby, in my arms. His legs drape over my arm; his head sways and wobbles. I kiss each one of his bare, muddy toes. I sing to him while the sewage sinks into my skin, and the sky grows dark. When his skin begins to cool, I blow on him the way the Nepali mothers taught me to do when the kids were ill. I try to pour my own life into his body, bathe him in it, bring his breath awake with mine, quench his eyes with my tears. His lips and fingernails start to turn blue. We rush him to the hospital where he has spent so much of his little, complicated life, but it's too late.

"My baby, my baby, my baby."

The sky begins to fall on us, illuminating him in a glorious orange glow and then pulling him into the dark. I pray for the white light, but there is none.

Ravi is gone. And I go away too.

12

DEAD PLANTS

Dear J,
When you get up to dance, we all follow.
—M

THE UNCLES WRAP Ravi's body in orange fabric and place him in a small box made of blond wood. I kiss his exquisite, pudgy cheek one last time and drop a bead of river water at his lips, the way the priest tells me to. In Nepal, the funeral rites begin as quickly after death as possible, before disbelief can mature into grief. Before you realize you're mourning your baby instead of loving him.

Birds chirp and banter all through the afternoon, like they know we're saying goodbye. Cuckoos and brown laughing doves sing mantras and eulogize, urging the earth to cover Ravi in protection. An old holy man walks clockwise around the gravesite with a stick of incense, moaning, caterwauling, eyes closed in concentration. More like a woman birthing a baby than a man burying one.

All of Kopila Valley huddles together, as men from the village dig the hole where Ravi will rest. The aunties and uncles are stoic for the children. The teachers from school and the artisans from the Women's Center weep softly. Tope and Kusum stand at the back, watching over me like a pair of golden hawks from the mountain. The kids are everywhere. I'm *with* them, shoulders brush shoulders, heads find their way to the comfort of my hip, but I don't really see them. I can't. There's just the box where Ravi sleeps in his new suit, hair brushed, lips still popsicle blue.

"Ravi, Raaaaavvi," I whimper to him, to the ghost of him, like we're back in our world of just two, our perfect place where every burp and chilly toe was its own miracle. Where love was the most extraordinary thing in the world, but also the simplest and most abundant.

I lunge toward the casket and press my cheek into the cold, smooth grain of the wood. Keshav grabs me around the waist like I'm a belligerent drunk and chaperones me back to the family. At eighteen, he's more a brother than a son.

"Shh," he whispers, gently holding me in his still-skinny arms and cradling the back of my head with his hand. My child holds and surrounds me as we sit on the dirt in the forest near Ravi's gravesite. When I see the children, I try to hold them too. "We're still a family," I say again and again and again. "We're still a family."

"Ravi."

It's the only language I have left. It's the answer to every question, the ultimate expression of joy, the cuss word, the lament. It's the greatest story ever told, and the worst.

"Ravi."

He had come to represent all of BlinkNow, everything about our whole mission. I'm not the first mother to lose her child. I know that. I've held on to women raging and melting to the ground the same way that I am. I've watched them, hands at their throats, trying to smother their own screams. I've shushed them, rocked them, tried to soothe the sorrow from their bodies. I've made them the empty promise that everything would be okay, that we would get through it together, not knowing that the word *together* had suddenly become nonsense. Nothing can be together when everything is missing.

My shoulders jerk up, and my lungs fill violently with the air I keep forgetting I have to breathe.

How could this have happened to us?

Why? Why? Why?

The priest's sad, old songs wax and wane, and they begin to lower the casket, so slowly, too slowly, into the ground. He dies a hundred times as he sinks inch by inch into the earth. My kids hold hands and fidget with their prayer beads. The ones who understand weep for Ravi, for me. The ones who don't try to squirm away from their boredom and full bladders. Their small, velvety voices stumble over mantras for their littlest brother, but they keep on. They believe that Ravi will come back to us. His soul will be born again and again, as a tree or a grasshopper or a kitten. They shut their eyes and find rest in the comfort that faith, never questioned and totally pure, can bring.

There is no comfort for me. Ravi was supposed to become a soccer player, a student, an astrophysicist—not a frog, not a patch of lichen or somebody's pet. Ravi was not an incarnation. He was my son.

I lift my head from Keshav's shoulder and try to look over at Ravi one last time, but the sun stings my eyes like it knows better. It's a mercy—the only mercy. I curl my body into Keshav and listen to dirt fall by heaps onto the straw-colored casket.

"Ravi. My baby. My baby. My baby. My baby."

"Everything will be okay," Keshav whispers. "Shh."

I GET THE sense that the kids are beginning to heal as the days draw on. They giggle and watch *The Chronicles of Narnia* and toot around on their bicycles in the driveway. They fight with each other and catch toads and practice making chords on the guitars they got for Christmas. I rely on it as some kind of proof that they are going to be okay. A tender new skin grows over the rawness. They pick up, they move on, color arriving in golds and pinks on the apples of their cheeks. While they learn fractions and pick lettuce from the garden, I can't lift a toothbrush or get to the toilet without help. I wonder if their youth or experience is the balm.

Anjali watched her parents die when she was six years old. Namraj was still warm from his mother's milk the moment when she left. We found Maya wild-eyed, orphaned, and alone. Life rolls in and out, a rhythm conducted by no one, tempted and influenced by nothing. Here, you lose your son or your mother, but you get the firewood, take care of the animals, carry the water, stoke the fire. If you're very lucky, you go to school. Grief is a horrible luxury afforded only to the privileged, and I don't deny myself.

I keep waiting to feel better, to feel something, but a week goes by and still I can barely open my eyes to receive the reality that I exist. Ravi's crib is still sidled up next to my bed, and a stack of soft, snowy diapers sit neatly on my shelf. Everything is a monument to him, not to be touched or moved. Ubji Auntie asks if she can tidy up for me, but I don't even answer her. I just lie there with Ravi's jammies over my face, searching for the faintest trace of him. Soon they smell more of my own breath than his.

The children who feel strong care for me the way I should be caring for them. Maya comes to my bedside in the mornings and wipes my tears away with tissue after tissue. Sagar tries to make coffee because he knows how happy coffee usually makes me. Namraj knits his body to mine at night, the way he used to when he was a baby, before Ravi ever was. I can't even speak to him, but he doesn't seem to expect it. He rests his cold feet on the backs of my calves and plays with my hair, while Sabita sings us "Castle on a Cloud" from *Les Misérables*. Ravi used to love her singing. I try to remember that she lost her brother—that they've all lost someone—but I can't see beyond my own grief.

Some of them are afraid of me. I don't blame them.

I'm scared for them too.

They tiptoe warily into my room to see how I'm doing, not totally sure of what state I'll be in. My cries find them in the middle of the night. They see the tender red lump on my head, throbbing and bloodied from bashing my skull into the wall. If they're brave enough to touch me, they feel bones where softness used to be.

Little Jhagat turns six a week and a half after the burial, and he won't come anywhere near me. He insists on holding Bauju's hand when I'm close by.

"You're *six*!" I choke out as joyfully as I can. I'm propped up on a plastic chair in the room we use for satsung.

I invite him to sit near me, but he doesn't want to. I have to bribe him with a remote-control helicopter and a bag of goodies. He gets closer and closer, eventually feeling bold enough to peek at his treasures.

"It's really for me?" he asks.

"Yes, it's for *you*!" I plaster on a smile and spin the plastic propeller, but I'm broken. I'm dead inside. All I can think about is Ravi. I'll never watch him tear open a gift or lick the icing from the bottom of his birthday candles.

The tears come, but I start to sing "Happy Birthday," motioning the others to join in. One by one, cautiously, they pick up the melody and carry it for me, the way they've been carrying everything since Ravi left. I haven't been able to look at them, but I see them now. I see chaos in a room designed to hold peace. I see *my* pain in their eyes, *my* sallow in their skin, *my* fear and exhaustion making little gray pillows under their eyes. They are the worst kind of mirror.

"Happy birthday, dear Jhagat," they yell, with more obedience than enthusiasm.

I can't take it.

My head falls into my hands; my knees fall to the floor. Jhagat runs away from me, and I don't see him for days.

Toughen up, I tell myself. *Be braver. Be stronger. Do it for the kids.*

I touch the bristles of a brush to the clods of hair on my head and take a sip of Sagar's terrible coffee. Then I see Ravi's tiny sneakers sitting by the door, still caked with mud from our last adventure, but now covered with a sheer blanket of dust. He's nowhere, yet he's everywhere.

I try to get up.

I try to be grateful.

I try to be a mom.

I fail.

My only job was to keep Ravi safe, and I failed.

———

I'M NOT SURE how much time goes by, less than two weeks maybe, but one day, Kate and my mom arrive at my bedroom door like a couple of specters, family I forgot I had, from an entirely different life. They pack up a suitcase with rumpled bits of clothing and fish my passport out of the drawer.

"We need to go home for a while," my mom announces as gently as possible from the foot of the bed. "We need to get you help."

Sweet Kate rubs the top of my hand until it starts to burn a little and pulls me up from the bed. I don't want to leave. *What kind of mother leaves her children?*

Jhagat peeks through the cracked door and blinks, his lashes forever and ever long. When our eyes meet, he shudders and takes off down the hall.

I've already left them.

My mom dresses me in leggings and an enormous "I Love Kopila" tee and then leads me out to the yard. Mechanically, I bow to place kisses on heads. I open and shut my arms and somehow utter the word *goodbye* like a piece of factory equipment. I don't say when I'll be back. I'm not sure that I will be. Kate sticks me in the sun, as she would a dead plant, before buckling me into the car, and then a plane just a couple of hours later. Gravity pushes me backward, and the bellow of the engines carries me off to sleep. I stay asleep for the next two weeks.

———

AFTER A FEW weeks of black, I'm standing again. I'm walking. I'm doing yoga stretches and listening to music. I read books, mostly about death and grief. But still, I can focus on the words; they don't spin or melt into each other. I can arrange them neatly in my mind. I've been in Chatham, a town right over from where my mom lives and right up the street from Ruth, for thirteen days.

The pain hits in momentary waves, some harder than others. It goes from being calm, to a ripple, to a hulking wall of blue that swallows me up and lands me on the bathroom floor, covered in vomit. There's no predicting it and no use trying to avoid it. I take out the recycling, and a tuna tin falls out. Ravi appears in a memory, whacking a can like a cowbell. I eat something mushy and remember starting him on solids, the way he rubbed rice all over his belly, how betrayed he was by the wedge of lemon that looked as sweet as the orange did. Sometimes I can survive the little dreams of him. I hang on to the edge of the countertop in the kitchen and let it wash over me. Other times, I throw up until there's nothing left in my stomach and spend an hour on the floor berating a God I'm not sure I believe in.

What kind of a God takes a child this way? If karma is real, where did I go wrong?

But then I think of my kids. Of Nisha watching a cancer eat her mother alive and . . .

What kind of God takes a mother before her child?

I've always believed that the universe was just. If there was a God, then God was good and fair. I behaved myself. I tried to do right. I loved my kids. None of it mattered. Ravi is gone. I nursed him from skin and bone into the fullest, brightest light in the world, and he's gone.

Why?

I expected the providence I paid for. It was promised to me in every children's story, every folktale and religious text. I know it doesn't work that way. Not everyone who suffers deserves pain. Not everyone who succeeds deserves to prosper. Life rushes in and it rushes out, without pause, reflection, or reward. I can't tell whether I need shelter with God or from him. I'm not sure if there's any God at all.

———————

THE DAYS ARE hard. The nights are harder. That was *our* time. I lie there with a couch pillow on my chest, where my baby should be, and I think about the river. I remember the trips we would take to our secret beach and try to re-create them in my mind. The kids spill out onto sand, bellies sore from the jeep's wonky suspension and the moguls on the road. One plunges in, then another, then me and Ravi. The water is ice and so blue with mineral you could paint with it. I let it shrivel the pads of our fingers and calm us with the noises it made simply being what it is: sloshing, gurgling, and lapping on the shore. Ravi loved the water. So did I. I bathed my babies at Bulebule and washed their clothing on the rocks. I drank from the life-giving spring on Maha Bua and let it soothe my broken skin. Long before Nepal, there was the bright white waterfall I found in the forest, and the pine-rimmed lake where I learned to swim. Hima and I found each other at the river. I lost Ravi in a little brown pool.

Why did he have to drown?

In my dreams, I pull him out of the water and rap him on the back. I dig him up out of the box in the ground and realize he was alive all along. He's not actually dead. He wakes up. But then I do too. He floats in every iridescent puddle on the street and in every glass of ice water that my friends force me to drink when they visit. The loss of him is so physical it has stolen my thirst. I loved water, but I can hardly stand the sight of it now.

My friends, our supporters, just about everyone I know texts and calls and stops by. I can't even bring myself to answer the phone or the door. I can't read sympathy cards or look at the flowers on the table. I can't open an email. My friend Megan is a therapist and trauma specialist, and at first, she's the only person I can bear to see.

She comes by to make sure I'm drinking enough and that I'm safe. When I stop sleeping and eating entirely, she makes an appointment with a therapist named Deb and practically carries me there.

The room smells like sandalwood and black tea and when I walk inside, I miss all my children, all at once. Deb is short and thin, and she wears a typical therapist's uniform: silk scarf, quirky earrings, a sweater that wants to be hugged.

"I'm happy you're here." She smiles at me, and I let her lead me over to her soft, gray couch.

"I'm so sorry," she says. "I'm so, so sorry." Settling in beside me, she presses a button on her oil diffuser, and it quickly hums itself to sleep on the side table. I miss the smell immediately.

"I lost my baby," I tell her.

"I know," she says. "I'm so, so sorry."

My Ravi.

Everything goes black, and before I can say anything, I'm screaming, an animal in a snare. I knock a book about landscape art off her coffee table and gasp and flail. She holds on to me with the strength and knowing of someone who has needed to be held before, and I bury my face into her cable-knit sweater, grabbing onto the thick ropes as if they'll save me from floating away.

"Shh," she whispers, just like Keshav did. I wait for her to promise me that everything will be okay. She doesn't.

A bowl of lentil soup appears from somewhere, in the corner, a benevolent, all-knowing soup god. I eye the rust-colored broth and think of drowning again, but she scoops me a spoonful, and I slurp it through my teeth. She makes me eat another spoonful and then one more. I feel stronger, so I try again.

"Ravi only ever wanted me. His entire face lit up whenever he could tell I was near. It was like nothing I've ever seen. He thought I was the funniest, most hilarious, most amazing person in the world. I didn't even have to do anything. Nothing. He said 'mama' over and over and over and over again. A love like that changes you."

Deb nods. "I'm so sorry. I know he was the love of your life. I lost the love of my life too."

She leans back into the sofa, takes off her glasses, and pinches the bridge of her nose as though she might cry too. "My husband." She smiles, maybe at a memory of him. "My boys were four and five. I thought I would die."

"I told my kids I *would* die if anything ever happened to them," I confess. "I said it a lot."

There's a long moment when we sit together and don't say anything. Somewhere in the silence, she becomes more of a friend than a stranger.

"How will I ever be okay again?" I ask. "How can I live?" I cry and shake.

For a moment, I see myself through her eyes: the matted hair, the enormous old sweatshirt draped over my skinny coatrack of a body, the range of pimples on my chin.

"I killed my plants last month." Deb sighs. "God, I loved those things."

My eyes glance to her again. Nobody has ever looked more like a person who adores her plants.

"I left the door open on the back porch when I was away for a long weekend. There was a snowstorm. The porch iced over, and by the time I got back from the trip, my plants were all brown and dead. Dead. Gone. They were completely gone. It didn't look like there was a cell of life left in them. My neighbor told me to throw them away, but of course, I couldn't. I just kept watering them and feeding them like I always had."

I have no idea where she's going, but I follow because she just spoon-fed me and let me wipe my nose in her hair.

"One day I saw a tiny green speck on the peace lily and a little bud," she says, "and I thought, *It's coming back again.* A piece of life. A little green speck. You have to find the little green specks inside of you. Find the speck, nurture it until it grows, until you feel alive again. The pain and the trauma and the grief will never go away but you will find your way to life again. You will feel joy. You'll laugh again. You won't get through this but you will continue on."

With the water back in my body and the sips of broth, I can sit up again. Megan appears in the doorway. We say goodbye, and I promise Deb I'll keep searching for the speck.

———

SLOWLY, VERY SLOWLY, comfort creeps in. Over the next few weeks, I decide to move from my dark bedroom to the small fireplace in my living room and the fluffy rug in front of it. I read Mary Oliver and Rumi and Hafiz instead of *Healing After Loss.* My friend Leslie comes over. She has a shovel and salt for my snowy porch. She has her homemade banana bread and more soup. She's organized every single email and condolence letter into a book and a binder. I find some words in my mouth, and I can talk to her. She lost her brother. I have found these past few weeks that it's only the women who have lived through the unspeakable who know what words to say. Everything else from anyone else cuts like a knife.

When my best friends show up at the door with Thai food and red wine, I let them in. I wear "the best gray sweatpants in the world" that they brought over for me and smell the bath bombs, laced with real lavender petals and patchouli. I fill the tub, which I swore I would never, ever do again, and stick my feet in, letting the warm liquid stroke my ankles. I stop yelling at my mom, and I journal instead. It's mostly cursing. I keep seeing Deb. She laughs at the jokes I can't believe I remember how to make, and we talk about grief, the lifelong epic shitstorm that we're in together. I tell her about my children, all fifty of them, and she listens. The chicken timer beeps for the soup she makes me one day, and I remember that I'm a mother.

Tope calls me on FaceTime that evening. All I can see when the screen flicks on is Bishal's enormous, steaming mouth.

"Maggie Mom! Maggie Mom! *Look!*"

He shoves a tiny, blurry sesame seed of an incisor at the camera.

"I lost my tooth!"

The kids start screaming. The screen wobbles, and the sound cuts out. It's Mardi Gras and Dashain combined. All because of Bishal's tooth. They're jumping and clapping and giggling until they fart. The aunties are pulling them off the furniture and each other and telling them to pack up their schoolbooks! Eat their breakfast! Brush their teeth! Bishal evades Kusum Auntie's glare, sticks his pointer fingers up in the air, and does a disco dance.

My eyes fill up. My body shakes. I laugh. Muscles in my stomach I thought had died come alive again in short, achy contractions. My cheeks burn. My lips crack as they stretch across my face, and I howl like a dog. I stick my finger up in the air and copy Bishal's moves. The sight of *me* dancing leads to an eruption of music and cheering and squeals. Maya jumps in front of the camera and knocks it with her pigtail, which is tied with a big, lime-colored ribbon.

My little green speck.

The next morning, I wake up, and I'm thirsty for the first time in a month.

13

ONE BRAVE THING

Dear Little B,
I miss you. The gap where your little front baby tooth is
missing makes my heart pitter patter. You are always so
brave.

—M

FOR JUST A week, a false spring softens New Jersey's stern, gray expression. Tender shoots of grass bust through the plates of ice that cover up the flowerbeds, and a few red-bellied birds manage to pry worms from the firmness of the earth. The sun is generous now, and I can see the roots of the trees again. I've missed them. Everywhere I turn, there is a little green speck, and I make myself look, though I don't really want to.

I have made a rule for myself that each and every day, I do one brave thing. Not necessarily a big thing, but a brave one. It's a promise I make that I hope will bring me back to myself and, eventually, to my kids and Nepal. Sometimes, bravery is taking a single breath when breathing feels defiant. Other times, it's answering the phone. When shame tells me one story:

If you had been watching him, he'd still be alive.

I tell myself another one:

You thought he was in safe hands.

I go to CVS one afternoon, when it's not busy, to practice being in the world with people. It feels like cliff diving. I sit in the plaza parking lot and peer out at the people. Everyone looks happy and busy, tucking wild carrot tops back into grocery bags, balancing cardboard carriers full of coffee, telling their waggly dogs to heel and stop sniffing every kid in a puffy coat that passes by. I watch and I wait behind the windshield, a fish in a bowl, not belonging in my container but not able to survive beyond it.

When I'm finally courageous enough to go inside the store, inevitably, there are babies everywhere—snoozing in strollers; squirming in carts, imprisoned by the plumpness of their own thighs; staring at me with wide, unblinking eyes and with webs of drool hanging from their lips. The stacks of diapers and baby shampoo make me groan out loud. I duck into the makeup aisle for a breath and pretend I want a tube of mascara. When that doesn't work, I pretend I want a pint of ice cream instead. I see *Are You My Mother?* at the checkout line, and I wonder if Ravi is looking for me somewhere, just like the little brown bird in the story.

The checkout guy is too friendly for me to keep up with. He asks me if I'm having a beautiful day, and I don't answer, but he doesn't seem to mind and whistles the melody of "You Can't Hurry Love" while he scans my gum.

There is so much I want to say to the world but can't.

"I promise, there's a reason I don't smile."

"I promise, there's a reason my eyes are all swollen."

"I promise this isn't me."

"I promise I'll say, 'Good afternoon' one day, but I don't even know how I'm standing right now."

Ravi is everywhere. He appears in the jar of peanut butter, the frozen raspberry bush, and the airplane in the sky. Grief can take any shape it wants to.

I find little safe places: the yoga room, Ruth and Hans's dining room table with their two teenage girls, who I try desperately to be strong for.

One day, my brave thing is to go over to the home of a beloved board member, Eileen Quick, and hold her brand-new grandbaby. It practically breaks me, but I don't feel envy or self-pity. Pulling out of the driveway, I'm proud of myself. I feel another speck inside of me come to life. I can hold a baby. I take long walks with Kim Wentworth and with Megan.

———

I HAVE TO go to Los Angeles in March. There's a mandatory training as part of our CNN Heroes contract. I use it as a deadline for my triumphant return to work. I'm nowhere near ready; it has been a few weeks since I lost my baby. Going to the pharmacy feels like an extreme sport, and my body won't let me eat anything but grapefruit. The tiny refrigerator in my apartment looks like the ball rack of a bowling alley. This is an existence, but not a life. It can't go on forever. I think of Nepali families losing their loved ones, waking up the next day for water and firewood, and carrying on with grief on their shoulders but rarely standing in their way.

I'm ashamed that I need this—the little apartment with the fireplace, the time off work, the therapy—but I do need it. I'm ashamed that I left fifty children in Surkhet and even more ashamed that everyone seemed to agree that I should leave. My children need me, even though I feel more like a vacancy than a mother. And I need them too. I have to get back there.

I promise Ruth I'll book the ticket, but as the days near, I can still barely get out of bed.

"There's no way," I tell her. "I can't go."

The last thing I want to do is leave the warmth of my home, the fireplace, the lavender diffuser, the little healing space I have made for myself, where no one can interfere. Ruth has been running the foundation for the past month. The aunties and uncles have been raising the kids.

"Maggie, you're booking your ticket, and you're doing it right now. You can do this. I know it," she argues. "California will be good for you. Visit friends! Let the sun shine on you for a minute."

America and Nepal are very different countries, but they agree on sunshine. I remember the sweet Nepali mamas in the villages oiling up their sniffly babies and laying them out in the sun to heal like a row of bikini models.

"I can't do it," I moan.

"You will. And you'll be great!"

Two days later, she helps me wad up my wardrobe into a suitcase, and she drops me off at the Newark airport.

"You can always come right back." Ruth smiles, holding my hands in hers and giving them a long squeeze. Her Subaru gives me a cheerful, cartoonish beep and rolls away. I'm alone with my hard-shell suitcase, the pit in my stomach, and a million fears.

THE AIRPORT WAS our place. We had to take numerous flights for surgeries and medical treatments. Most people dread traveling with a baby, but I loved flying with Ravi. He enjoyed the buzz of suitcase wheels rumbling along the moving sidewalk and the ear-splitting loudspeaker announcements that always made us jump and seemed to come out of nowhere. We spent forever browsing the souvenir shops, with their snow globes and refrigerator magnets and stuffed bears in "I Love New York" or Dubai or Helsinki crop tops. He made everybody everywhere smile. At first, everyone would look at me with pity, fumbling with trays at security check and trying to shove the stroller through the X-ray machine—*that poor mom, traveling all alone with a baby*—but they'd watch him for a minute and understand. It didn't take more than that to fall under Ravi's spell, to realize that he was magic, unlike any other baby or any other person in the world. The memories come back all at once. It feels so wrong to be here without him.

I feed my passport into the United Airlines kiosk, and it asks me if I'm "traveling with an infant." Pain shoots through my gut and all over my body. With every ounce of strength I have, I press "No."

Doubled over, I make my way to the gate, buy the first coffee I've had in months, and use a fresh copy of *The Girl on the Train* like blinders until the final boarding call.

Get on the plane.

Get on the plane.

GET ON THE PLANE, MAGGIE!

One brave thing, I remind myself. *Just one brave thing at a time.*

CALIFORNIA IS WHATEVER you need it to be, as rich in red wine as it is in ocean water, home of the Lone Cypress and the Muir Woods. You can find yourself here or pretend to be somebody else entirely. I do the latter. The sidewalks and restaurant patios are lined with wannabe actors ready to make believe, to disappear into a new life. I'm just another one.

I stay in a no-nonsense hotel on Sunset, not far from an IHOP and the CNN building, which is giant and made of black glass and looks at any time like it could release an army of stormtroopers. There's a silver vat of coffee in the hotel lobby, and the morning of the training, I spend an hour pouring cup after cup, until my armpits begin to sweat, and my heart is flickering. I work out in the small gym, dragging my body forward on the rowing machine and kicking it back until I have enough serotonin and caffeine in my blood to power through the day.

I can't survive being Ravi's mom, so I put on a costume from Ann Taylor LOFT and pull my hair into a bun so tight my eyebrows jump up to the base of my scalp. I don't look like Maggie Doyne. I look like somebody who uses a cigarette holder and wants to make a coat out of puppies.

"One brave thing at a time," I remind myself in the mirror. Though I'm not sure how brave it is to hide behind a wall of khaki.

The person I become that day belongs in the fancy conference room at the nonprofit training at the Annenberg Foundation, with the swivel chairs and the huge binder and the free bagels. She listens to people talk about life-changing hamburgers and spinning classes, and she can even nod along like she cares. Yes, she will try the animal-style french fries, and no, she's never done yoga on a stationary bike. She's fun to be around, and she has great ideas. She didn't just lose her son, but I did. Nobody here knows that Ravi is gone except for Libby Delana and Patty, who are at the training with me and stay hunkered down on either side of me for the day, squeezing my hands under the table, reminding me to take breaks and drink water. We talk about the work that I do, and from a distance, in my work clothes and my makeup, removed from who I really am and everything in my heart, I can be excited for the future. At the end of the day, I see the next five years clearly, but I don't know how I'm going to get past the pictures of children in the office hallway and back down to the ground floor. I'm equally proud of my acting and horrified by it.

In the elevator, my knees buckle, and I cry out for Ravi. Libby and Patty each grab an elbow and walk with me back to the hotel. In the midst of living two lives, I'm not living at all.

———

AFTER THE FIRST day, Libby asks me to come meet up with her and some of the people she works with at a place called the Soho House. Libby is a branding genius, and they just finished a shoot for something or other. The day has an endless number of hours, and eventually, I surrender to it, showing up when and where the text messages tell me to. I pull on my next costume, which is flimsy compared to the previous one, old jeans and some lip balm. Even my own lips remind me of Ravi, of covering him in kisses and singing him his favorite songs. The phone blinks at me with a message: *Come to the Soho House at 8 tonight.*

The kids call on FaceTime before I leave. They're just waking up in Surkhet, and Bishal's hair is sticking up in six different directions. For a moment, I'm a mom again. We talk about *chungi*, a game they like to play in the yard with a ball made of strips of an old tire. It's basically a Nepali version of Hacky Sack. Yagay is good at it now, and Namraj is starting to play. Most of the girls are bored by it, except for Maya, who sticks her face in front of the camera.

"When are you coming home?" she demands, smiling devilishly like she wants to calculate how much time she has left to cause trouble.

"I don't know, Maya."

"I love you, Mom."

"I love you too." I just barely choke it out. The words are blessing and omen.

I love you, Maya. But I don't ever want to lose you.

Of all the brave things, the airport and the meetings and the trips to CVS, saying "I love you" is the bravest.

———

I STEP OUT of the hotel, into the oranges and pinks of early evening. Patty and I head to meet up with Libby and her work friends. I pass a cell phone store and a kinky lingerie place, where the mannequins have collars on, so they don't escape the storefront. Palm fronds shiver in a flawless Hollywood breeze, and I could cry as cool air gently strokes my hair and whispers things I can't make out but that comfort me anyway. Important people scatter from the office buildings, buttoned into costumes of their own, cell phones perched on their shoulders in the places where, later, a child might ride or a lover might rest. It's a big, lonely mob, and I wonder if anyone else is just carrying on, like I am. I want to stop the suits that brush by me and ask:

Are you going home?

Is there somebody waiting for you?

Are you sure you don't already have everything you're looking for?

Go home. Go now, if you have it in you.

A gaggle of long-legged models gather and preen outside the bars like tall wading birds. Their eyes drift to the men walking by. I watch them touch their hair and point their toes, and I want to stop them too.

Love isn't a puzzle you can solve.

It doesn't come in pieces.

Love is the wholeness.

Love is what holds everything else together. Until it's gone.

Laughter rolls from them in a low thunder. They touch their pink, boozy cheeks and hold their bellies. I think of Ravi. I find him on billboards and in grains of sand, in bathroom stalls and in crossword puzzles. How can he be gone and still be so alive in the world? Am I standing in his shadow or his light? How can I move forward when all I want is to remember?

Ravi is everywhere, but Bishal, Pabitra, and Namraj have begun to show up too. In the kite at Venice Beach, electric pink and crumpled like a cheap princess gown, in the commercials for Olive Garden's all-you-can-eat spaghetti, in the lone papaya at the Jamba Juice. Anjali is in yoga class, and Goma is in every Justin Bieber song. Sundar is in the USA Network's presentation of *Saturday Night Fever*, and Maya is in Libby's copy of *I Know Why the Caged Bird Sings*. I see Juntara, too, every single time I drink a glass of cool water. I remember the spring she took me to in Odanoku, the way she combed the morning mist with her fingers and the sound of the big, booming mountain singing back to her. She's in the letter that lives on the back three pages of my journal, that I wish, more than anything, she'd been able to read.

I left my children.

I need to get back to them, but I don't know how.

As the last bits of color drain from the sky and the streetlights flash on, Patty and I find Soho House, step onto an elevator, and ride up.

IT'S SWANKY, THERE'S a buzz of noise, and everyone's wearing leather and heels and red lipstick, and I feel like a fish out of water. Patagonia jackets and Soho House don't go together. I missed the memo. I feel the hostesses behind their stand looking me up and down. I swear they're about to ask me for the secret code word. *Is that what they do at cool bars? Why did I come here? What am I doing?*

I'm holding on to Patty, hoping she can speak for the two of us and justify our presence. Then I see a huge staircase and a man dressed in black, walking down toward me and saying my name.

It's him.

Jeremy is a filmmaker. I met him at the Do Lectures, where I gave a talk last year. I definitely felt an instant pull and friendship with him when we met, but days later, I'd left for Nepal. We always said we'd meet up again, but I didn't expect it to be like this. He's tall and bearded and Canadian and looks more like a man who makes his own maple syrup than a man who makes movies. He had wanted to shoot a documentary about Kopila Valley, and every few months, he'd sent me an email or text with seventeen new ideas. I've ignored most of them.

He's waving like he's lost in a crowd.

"Maggie!" he calls, raising his hand to his mouth like a bull-horn, still convinced I'm going to miss him, as the music with too much bass blares around us. He says it again:

"Maggie!"

In the Soho House, in LA, the smell of vodka hanging in the air, the costume falls away from me. Don't worry—I still have my clothes on, but I'm myself, and I'm smiling, truly smiling, at a person I hardly know for reasons I can't explain. The only explanation is nonsense, but the way he stands, the arrangement of his things: keys, phone, wallet, neatly grouped together on the table, make me want to laugh and cry and dance. Grief can take any shape it wants to, but maybe so can love.

"Hi, Jeremy."

The plates inside me begin to shift, and I beg them not to. It's a little bit like meeting Hima in the riverbed and a little bit like seeing my oldest friend. It's like having Ravi on my chest and listening to Juntara sing to her family's buffalo. The man across the room is important. I hate the way I feel, but I can't help but feel it. There hasn't been room in my heart for one more person for a long time, and there isn't room now. Love is a matter of fact, not choice.

I cross the room, and the closer I get to him, the closer I feel to myself. For a moment, the pale green speck I've been tending becomes an overgrown valley, dense and joy-filled, with a slow-moving river and a perfect white house, guarded by a company of pine-covered mountains and low-hanging clouds.

Smiling through his dark scruff, as strangely happy to see me as I am to see him, he opens his arms. There is so much I want to say:

I'm scared.

I'm broken.

I lost my baby.

Instead, I let somebody hold me. It feels like the brave thing, the honest thing. It's more than a friendly hug—it's a knowing one. I sink into it. He's warm, safe, and steady, rooted to the moment like a tree.

"It's good to see you," he says.

It's good to be seen.

14

LOVE LETTERS

Dear Y,
You and I play this game. I say, "You are my heart."
Without skipping a beat, you say, "You are my air." I say,
"You are my moon." You say, "You are the all the stars in
the sky."

—M

J EREMY POWER REGIMBAL grew up on a farm in Livelong, Saskatchewan. He has five siblings, and his parents are loving, white-haired hippies who live on a beautiful island in British Colombia now. He's happy and successful, always curious and never fearful. He makes commercials for running shoes and classy sedans during the day and crafts beautiful tables from big blocks of wood on his back deck at night. I like everything about him: his apartment in Echo Park, the way he drinks his coffee, his happy black dog, Bear, who is almost as crazy about him as I am. He's never lost anyone close to him before, and I worry that he'll never understand me.

Our first date is a road trip to the desert. He asks me to go with him and we leave two days later in his Jetta, Bear the dog planted between us on the center console. I make a game of telling myself I don't love Jeremy, every time I see a green sign or a Joshua tree or a ball of garbage. But I know that I do, for reasons I can't explain but am absolutely certain of.

I love him when he can't find a radio station that he likes and when his jealous dog pants hot, sour breath onto my neck. I love the pink sunburn stretching across his nose and the sturdy, black-rimmed glasses he wears. It's too much too soon, and I know it, but I've become a mother overnight fifty times. I've never been wrong about love, even when it's hurt me.

We spend the day hauling our bodies up white rocks as big as whales and standing under granite arches. He reaches his hand out for mine; I grab hold. He reaches out again and again, whether I need him to or not. We slither up the dust-slick sides of the giant stones and stare out over the unending bareness of the earth, not needing words for comfort but talking anyway. The air is so dry here that it steals the tears from my eyes and sweat from my skin, but still flowers grow, appearing like magic in the scrub. Pink pom-poms explode from cactus paddles, and black-eyed lilies peek out from the brush. Jeremy points them all out, like he's trying to prove to me that the world can be beautiful.

"It's so empty," I say, leaning into his body at the top of a stony hump.

"There's so much *space*." He smiles back at me, hopping down and reaching back for me again. Bear trots ahead of us to stare down the cholla cacti and bark at snake-shaped bits of brush. We walk for hours, listening to the metronomic scrape of our feet on the ground and talking about all the glorious little things, the way the sky looks, and our favorite kinds of peanut butter.

With every saguaro cactus, incomprehensible Tom Waits song, and skittering roadrunner, gravity feels less like a boulder strapped to my back. I can breathe. I can laugh, deep, quaking laughs that course all the way through me. We joke and play and kiss until we're as weightless as the tiny sandstorms that swirl up at our feet.

But inevitably, I remember. I find Ravi in the blueness of the sky or the word *potato*. He never could pronounce the *p*.

Then, I can't imagine loving Jeremy without mourning Ravi.

"What are you thinking about?" I ask him a few times when we've settled into our thoughts, as the sun sinks, the air cools, and Bear's breath becomes happy little clouds in the dark.

"What if there was a movie about . . . ?" He goes on and on about a beautiful story he's imagined, or an invention, or the real estate market. Jeremy knows what happened with Ravi, but he doesn't bring it up all day. I nod and listen, terrified of pulling him too close, pushing him away, or losing him altogether. The only story I can tell myself is of a mother who lost her son.

It can never work, I tell myself over and over.

Our car gets a flat tire at the edge of a wind farm, just as the sun sinks and the air cools on our arms. I stand under the hulking turbines and watch the last of the day's shadows spin across his face.

You're not ready, my fussy mind scolds my heart relentlessly.

But in the darkest dark, he reaches out for me again.

———

I SPEND THE next four weeks in Los Angeles, falling in love with Jeremy. I move in with my friend Roda, who I met in NYC years ago when I was visiting with Anjali. I knew we'd be a match when she took us to Times Square in the middle of the night to reenact Anjali's favorite scene from *Enchanted*, when the princess pops out of the sewage hole. There was something about Roda that transformed ordinary moments into magic.

In LA, Roda drops everything in her life to help me heal mine. She gets me out of bed in the mornings and makes me go to a hot yoga class in a strip mall, where we spend ninety minutes pretending to be trees and trying not to vomit on ourselves. She makes a rule that I'm only allowed to cry for five hours per day (I cheat in the shower) and gently reminds me that I might like to do things like brush my hair and chew a stick of gum before Jeremy takes me out for a margarita.

With or without tragedy, all of it is new to me. I'm a mother of fifty on hiatus, grieving, usually living in a remote region but suddenly in the most famous city in the world. The sexiest item I've worn to bed in the past year is a puffy vest. And it's mauve. Life hasn't been filled with romance, and I've never expected a partner. However, in the slow-sinking afternoons, where we have nowhere to be but with each other, nothing to do but walk circles around the lake at Echo Park, with its giant, swan-shaped paddle boats, I know I've found one.

In the evenings, we sit by the fire, and I notice more glorious little things: the soft grain in the wool of the sweater Roda lent me, the spitting sound that the flames make, the perfect weight of Jeremy's hand on mine. I miss Ravi so much it crushes me, but I like not missing him alone. Jeremy knows how to comfort me. When I need fresh air or might need to lie down, he talks me through the most irrational of my fears:

"What if I'm never funny again?"

"What if I never sleep through the night?"

"What if the old Maggie is gone?"

"What if I never love another person?"

"You love me." He smiles and winks. "And you love your kids too."

I do love them. Wildly. They seem more grown up every night when I talk to them. Nisha is going to college soon, and Dipak learned to make chocolate cake. Madan says the buildings are sprouting at our new green school, and Namraj wants to know if I'll be back for the Holi festival at the end of March. All I can say is what I have been saying:

"I don't know. But I love you."

And it's the truest thing. My fear of love has never diminished my capacity for it.

I wonder at times, though, if I even should go back to Surkhet. Though he'd never admit it, Tope is managing Kopila Valley amazingly, even in the midst of his own grief. The kids are thriving with Sachyam and Aakriti, the newest members of the caregiving team. The love that I wanted to bring to those children, they have in abundance.

What am I now?

Another person who left them?

Another white kid who tried to fix a country and left when things got hard?

A hypocrite?

A failure?

Still, awake at night in the arms of a man I adore, I'm pulled back to the green, green valley and the kites in the sky, to the children who made me a mother and the land that made me a woman. Kopila Valley is my home. And it's calling for me.

————

ONE MONTH INTO love, Jeremy and I take a road trip from California to Canada, where his family lives. If our relationship can survive two weeks in his tiny car filled with dog breath, the rest will be a cakewalk. Bear retreats to the back seat and curls up like a roly-poly bug, and we start off on the Pacific Coast Highway. The traffic thins, and the city shrinks into a blanket of smog behind us as we head north toward Big Sur, weaving between long-haul truckers and sixty-year-old men in brand-new convertibles. Travel has always been hard: days of trekking; a frantic scramble from the terrible hospital in Surkhet to the less terrible hospital in Nepalgunj to the excellent hospital in Kathmandu; the long, bumpy bus rides with their broken windows and chickens pecking at the floor. With Jeremy, travel is almost something that happens *to* me. I tuck my legs into my chest like Bear and watch the islands as they pop up in the sea.

I talk more than either of us expect (I'm sure), but Jeremy listens, whether I'm laughing at one of his many ridiculous jokes or moaning because Ravi is gone. Most days, I do both. He listens to every little thing, as the car climbs above mighty slabs of volcanic rock and the ocean stares back at us. I still can't stand the water, even when it's turquoise and frothy and perfect. A drop of rain can bring Ravi's death back in technicolor. When I'm struggling, Jeremy asks me questions.

"Tell me what you were like when you were little," he says, as we hike along the poppy-rimmed path at Point Lobos.

"I played soccer and loved my sisters."

"Tell me about your parents," he says, ducking between rows of dark-skinned grapes in Mendocino.

"They're divorced. It might be my fault."

Then, as the redwoods rise up out of the ground, and everything, absolutely everything from the moss on the rocks to yellow-bellied meadowlarks, seems to stop to listen, he asks me to tell him about the kids.

I share it all with him. I talk about walking home with Nisha when she was six years old and teaching her the words for "tree" and "fence." I talk about Madan breaking his arm and Yagay losing his first tooth. I tell him about Shanti refusing to talk for the first six months and Sagar refusing to cut his hair. I talk about Ravi for a long time, and I don't cry quite as much as I normally do.

"Do you remember him?" I ask, almost shyly. They met fleetingly, many, many months ago, not far from the olive orchards and dirt roads we're driving on.

"Of course." He smiles and grabs my hand.

It feels good to remember Ravi with someone, to have somebody agree that his nose was perfect and that he was deliciously fat. When I tell him that I replay Ravi's death in my head sometimes ten or fifteen times a day, that I hate the water, and that he should be just as afraid of love as I am, he reaches out for me again.

"Tell me about Shova," he says, and together, we walk through the deep green shadow of the forest. There are thousands of glorious little things to tell him, and he wants to picture each one in his mind. I do too.

When we get back to the car, I take out my journal and start writing a love letter. I haven't written a letter to anyone since I lost Juntara.

Dear Little B,

I miss you. The gap where your little front baby tooth is missing makes my heart pitter-patter. I remember the night I yanked it out. You are always so brave.

I love how your hair is still fine and baby soft. I love watching you ride your bicycle and play and get right in the

*mix with all your big brothers. I love your kind and sensitive
side and most of all I love you you you.*

Xoxo,
Mama

I write another:

Dear Bhatka,
You have the most beautiful, enduring, resilient spirit.
*You are also the most stubborn human being I've ever met
in my life.*

xo,
Mom

And another . . .

Dear Sagar,
*I'm sorry I made you cut your hair. I'm really sorry. You
loved your hair, and I made you cut it, and it wasn't a cool
move. "I love my hair more than I love girls," you told me.
And you really, really LOVE girls. You are growing into a
strong, kind, beautiful young man, and I'm blessed to
watch you.*

xo,
Mom

I spend the next two days lost in the adulation of Sundar's hustle,
Asmita's bedhead, and the way Ganga dances in the rain. Jeremy
drives north, past the ragged cliffs to where the sand darkens,
and California becomes the Pacific Northwest. I tell him more
and more about the children, and I fall deeper in love—with him,

them, and the ache of life. Home calls out to me, and I begin to answer back.

We arrive at Cannon Beach after four days on the road, and something in me is different. I look out onto the silver of the ocean, and I see Bulebule. I remember the way our clothing rumbled across the rocks, as I washed it with bar soap and every ounce of muscle I had. The sunshine practically sprays from the sky onto the wet black sand and covers everything, including me, in pale morning light. I can feel Ravi with me, in a sudden burst of rapture. I open the car door and leave Jeremy still sipping his coffee and checking his Google Maps.

Careening down a treacherous path toward a brood of smooth rocks as big and holy as the stupas in Nepal, I come alive. I'm no longer consumed with love and grief—I'm in awe of them. Bear canters along behind me, releasing a stern string of woofs, but I don't slow for him. The wind is blowing hard, and I let it lead me into a cove. I lean my body into the gusts and let the air hold the things that have gotten too heavy—the guilt, the shame, the memories. Bear catches up, and we dance together, twirling in circles as I laugh, sprinkles of sand arriving between our teeth and eyelashes. Jeremy watches from the foot of the path a distance back, cracking up and holding his belly.

Hair lashes against my face. The air tastes like brine, but even eight thousand miles away, I feel so close to home. I see the river beach, the temple, the curtains of rain that come during the monsoon season. A dark wedge of stone sits far out in the water. It's a pebble compared to the green mountains I've slept beside for the past ten years, but when I sing and laugh, it sends my voice back to me, just as they do. The water, cold as winter, is a plain that stretches on and on, crawling up onto shore and retreating.

Life rushes in and it rushes out, carrying bits of the bedrock away forever, molding the earth like a ball of putty. There is no freedom from it—only in it.

Slowly, with all the trust and faith I can muster, I walk into the icy water that I hate, and I try to love it. I let it lap against my ankles. I cry out for my baby because he's gone. Bear nips at the surf as it comes from the ocean to chase him, and Jeremy wraps his arms around me. Life rushes in and it rushes out. Love is all that remains.

———

WE GO TO Portland to visit my sister Kate and my friends Cheryl and Lauren, who are so excited to see me in love that they blush and pour too much wine and are almost embarrassingly supportive. I'm shocked that they don't find a way to get Jeremy and me married before we leave. We continue north—toward the border, stopping to watch slick, ink-colored seals spin through the water—to find more tall forests to keep our secrets. I keep writing to my children, a bit more every day. Jeremy decides that he'll come back to Nepal with me to meet them.

Dear Anjali,
You love big and intensely. Your giggle is contagious, and as much as I love your serious and driven artist side, I love when you're silly. I love when you keel over laughing and have to gasp for breath. I hope I get to watch you laugh like that forever and that you always remember all the reasons you have to smile. Your smile is killer, even with the braces you got this year. You rock them so well.

Love,
Maggie Mom

Dear Manisha,
Whenever I can't fall asleep at night, I think about your smile
and try to play your giggle on repeat over and over again in
my head. Your laugh is the best sound in the entire world,
and you fill our home with it each and every day as part of
the Kopila soundtrack. You are magic. Know how loved you
are, always. And never ever ever lose that sparkle in your eye.
  Love you to the moon.

Mommy

Dear Yagay,
You have the most incredibly winning smile that always gets
me. It takes you a while to open up until your huge dimpled
grin betrays you. There are really no words to tell you how
proud it makes me to be your mom. It's better than winning
the lottery or the biggest prize in the world. And each day
you get older, you turn into a more amazing little boy. I
admire you and love you and look up to you. I kind of want
to be you.
  Thanks for letting me be your mom.

Xoxoxo

We arrive in Canada on a sleepy ferry just before lunchtime, after a full week on the road. Looking out over the ocean and toward Vancouver Island, Jeremy's brother Jesse points out the diving birds and tells me where and when they've spotted the orcas. The horn blares, which delights the tourists on board, and Jeremy's parents appear as tiny waving blips on the dock.

"Are you ready?" he asks, wrapping me in the peace of his arms.

I smile and wave back to them.

They are there with three more of the five Regimbal brothers and sisters waiting to pick us up in their old Red Durango on Vancouver Island. They look like the best folk band of all time and love me immediately. We ride together to watch Jeremy's three little nieces at a soccer game. Inexplicably, I feel close to home again. Jeremy's family is kind and tender and funny, exactly as I imagined them. Every glorious little thing he told me is true.

15

THE NEW LAND

Dear K,
From the moment I saw you, I knew you belonged in our
family. It was instantaneous.

—M

T HE SKY CHANGES as we enter Nepal. Two white peaks split
through the clouds, jagged and glimmering like uncut stones.
I notice them from the airplane window, those same two, almost
every time I come or go. I don't remember seeing them when I left
with Kate and my mom. I hardly remember leaving at all, just the
feeling of being gone.

Jeremy leans over in his seat and fixes his camera on the two
mountain signposts, capturing the boundary between my world
and the rest of it. I'm home. *We* are home. My ears fill with pressure as we drop lower in the sky. I open my journal and write a
letter to my daughter.

Dear Maya,
The day you came, I looked into your eyes and felt
overcome by love. You needed a name, and it rolled off the
tip of my tongue. "I'm going to name her Maya!" I told
everyone proudly. It was the first time I ever got to choose
a name on my own, and it seemed to suit you so well.

"Maya" means "love" in Nepali, and you are one of the biggest loves of my life.

xo,
Mom

The wheels stretch out with a groan from the steel belly of the plane, and it hits me: I made it.

Tope meets us at the airport in a small open-air hallway that smells like jet fuel and dust. We hold on to each other for a long, silent stretch of time, trading deep breaths that rise up from underneath our shoulder blades. In the quiet, I write a letter for him too.

Dear Tope ji,
You're everything I hope the children will be.
  Thank you for leading when I could barely breathe.
  Thank you for teaching and guiding me all these years.

I love you.
—Maggie

A cuckoo hollers at us from the hibiscus tree in the courtyard. I wipe my eyes and giggle from the delirium and relief of being home again. Tope and Jeremy share a sweet, awkward hug, and together we walk toward the sizzling parking lot and climb into the truck.

The sky is dark when we roll past Surkhet's dry paddies and through the front gates of Kopila Valley. The kids should be asleep, but they're awake and everywhere, jumping and crying and cheering, singing six different songs in four different keys, bickering about who gets to stand where. Little Bishal sticks his tongue out at Yagay, and Maya pouts at Sabita. Pabitra and Khajuri release shrill little-girl squeals that make the neighborhood dogs howl, and I love them all so much my stomach hurts. I feel a sense of relief I haven't felt in a long long time.

The big boys lift me and spin me around, and the little ones jump on my back like they're playing a sport that nobody understands. After three months away, their breath is the sweetest, freshest air, and "Mom! Mom! Mom!" is music.

Jeremy is standing by the truck and smiling, soaking up the chaos and joy. He's nearly two feet taller than anybody else, and he's already started to sweat through his shirt.

"Guys, this is Jeremy," I sputter.

"Hiiiii," they sing at him.

I sink to my knees and comb my fingers through the dry, hopeless dirt where I thought nothing could grow. I look around, left and right, at everything and everyone: children, aunties, uncles, hope, joy, family, love, peace. Fifty perfect faces, illuminated by love, shine down onto me.

Dear Namraj,
When you fall asleep next to me, you curl up in a ball and
find a way to wrap your arms and legs around me and nuzzle
your head into my neck and make sure we are completely
intertwined . . .

Dear Jhagat,
Your sweetness is too much for me to handle. Every time I see
you, I just want to run up and give you a squeeze.

Dear Manisha . . .

Dear Sundar . . .

I place my hands together in prayer. Bauju places tikka on my forehead and lays a necklace of yellow marigolds around my neck. I step back and watch Jeremy bow down to do the same. He smiles at me, face streaked with red rice powder, neck adorned with blush-colored petals. I'm so in love with him, so profoundly and pitifully in love. He rises to his feet, and cheers roll through the yard, past the gate, and out toward the green mountains. Faintly, I hear them sing back to us. Peace settles over me. This is not where I was born, but it is where I come alive.

––––––

FOR A FEW days, I call Jeremy "my friend."

"He's here to shoot portraits of you!" I tell the children. "And to take drone footage of the new school!"

Even the littlest ones roll their eyes.

I could call Jeremy "my rhinoceros," and they'd know what was going on. My cheeks grow hot and pink when I see him come down for breakfast in the morning. Our knees lean comfortably into each other under the table, at soccer games, during satsung. Goma keeps grinning and telling me how happy I look. She knows; they all do. If they don't, they figure it out when the Nepali police cart him off to the station for flying his drone without a permit. I hop in the police car with him and act as a translator as they confiscate the drone, all his footage, and take his mug shot. The whole thing makes viral national Nepali news. (Don't worry—they gave him back to us after forty-eight hours and a trip to Kathmandu to pay a fine at a government office there.)

What the children don't know is that Jeremy is falling in love with them. I see it in the funny faces he makes for Namraj and in the way he swings Little Bishal onto his shoulders just one more time before bed. I see it in the thousands of pictures he seems to take, of Shanti getting ready for school and Padam on the motorbike, of the goats and the sunflowers and the fog, as though he wants to remember every flower and freckle and fern exactly. I see it in how badly he wants to freeze time, just like I do.

Over the next year, Jeremy travels back and forth from Surkhet to the US, where he shoots commercials for cars and shampoo and sweatproof makeup. I miss him terribly, but I keep healing and writing my letters, freezing time the best way that I know how.

Dear Khajuri,
You're the embodiment of all things good and pure. You are resilience and strength. You are a diamond that emerged from the most unexpected place . . .

Dear Bindu,
You are so special. I've never met another human being like you. I know you are here to make magic. I can't wait to be a witness . . .

Dear Kalpana,
One of my greatest blessings was knowing your mother. You remind me so much of her it takes my breath away . . .

Slowly, though gratitude never dwarfs grief, the two begin to stand together. I can go to the river again. I can walk down the stairs without seeing Ravi there in the auntie's arms. I can sing the songs he used to love at satsung. I am able to save my deep sobs to the nighttime long after the kids are asleep. We sit in family circles and talk about our loss and I tell the kids it's okay to say his name. I promise them over and over again it was not their fault that he died. Dreams begin to come to me again in the bed that we shared.

During the day, when the children are at school and the house feels too empty, I throw myself at the new school construction site, diving straight into the promise of it, inspecting every pebble, memorizing every leaf shape, and tasting the sweetness of each fruit that bows the branches in the orchard. I sit in on meetings with the best and brightest minds in the world and feel slightly out of place in all of their structural engineering and architectural talk. Instead I point to my Pinterest board, why we are doing what we do, and the vision of how I want the kids to feel when they walk onto the campus. On Saturdays, the kids come with me, and together, we marvel over what we're building: rammed-earth buildings that stand like copper titans around the courtyard, twigs we planted with our own hands becoming trees, great green gardens. We step into the classrooms to feel the cool of the floors on the soles of our feet and stick our heads, dwarfed by banana yellow hard hats, out from the lovingly carved places where the windows will sit. We watch the solar panels arrive, straight from the future, glinting and blinding, and *oooh* and *ahhh* as they're fixed to the places that they belong. I wax on and on about aquaponics, permaculture, rainwater collection, biogas, agroforestry, and Prabal, our architect. Together, we watch new seasons wash over the meadow, changing it from brown to gray to green.

"It's going to be the best school in Nepal!" we yell, listening to the sound of our voices fly over the land, snacking on tender lettuces and stroking the cows' damp, pink noses. It is going to be the best school. I believe it.

———————

Jeremy comes back in the springtime, when everything is lush and the leaves are bright and as tough as cowhide. We steal away to the campus at dusk to watch the sun set over the pasture where the new animals graze, staring out at the hillscape. The distance between us has been possible only because we're crazy for each other, only because we're constantly dreaming of when our life together can truly begin and imagining what it will look like when it does. One night, deep in love and gazing into my eyes, Jeremy tells me he wants to have a baby together. With more sincerity in his eyes than I've ever seen, he says that he doesn't want our biological child to miss all this.

Is he ready to stay in Nepal?

Are we ready to get married?

Jeremy wants to have a baby and part of me does too. Am I sure I'm ready?

The idea of having a child, carrying a child, makes me sweaty and nervous. Ravi was my baby. He's gone now. The sacred store of devotion I kept for him, that all mothers keep for their babies, died when he did, but I've watched love grow from dust before. As Jeremy sits next to me on the knoll, light falling perfectly on his face, casting gold over the eyes that held me steady and the lips that sang me to sleep, I want to know our baby. Even though I can hardly bear it.

The night before Ravi's third birthday, I sit in my room, staring out into the thicket of stars that used to shine down on us. Jeremy is asleep, snoring softly under the mosquito net, all sprawled out.

It's time to write to Ravi.

Dear Ravi,

Sweet baby of my heart. This is killing me. This is the last thing on the planet I would have ever wanted. I want you here, lying on my chest like you always were. I want to be stroking your hair and kissing your cheeks or splashing in the bathtub together. I want you in our BabyBjörn, going on adventures, and in the grocery cart, shopping for dinner, and playing with your forty-nine brothers and sisters. I love you more than I've ever loved anyone or anything. You taught me the deepest kind of love I've ever known. I miss you so much, the word "miss" won't ever feel enough, and all the wishing, hoping, and praying in the world won't bring you back.

When I can't sleep and the pain feels like too much, I try to go back in time to that day when I took off from work and we drove over to the farm and watched the ponies and the goats. You giggled at the top of your lungs every time the goats jumped up over the fence and ate out of our hands. Then we walked through the sunflower maze, with a few thousand of the biggest sunflowers I'd ever seen. We went and picked raspberry after raspberry after raspberry. Your chubby cheeks were covered in them. You were eating them faster than I could pick them, and I thought we were going to get in trouble because you're not supposed to eat the berries until after you pay. Then we went and played in the peach orchard, eating peach after peach after peach. We sat under the peach tree while you practiced your crawling and your standing and giggled some more. I take myself back to underneath that peach tree. I remember how happy we were.

I actually remember thinking there, in that moment, that it was the happiest I had ever been in my entire life.

I remember you and I reenacting the scene from Lady and the Tramp *. . . you with one end of the noodle and me with the other, and how you would laugh and laugh. I remember dancing with you every single day. How you loved music and shaking your booty to it.*

You were the best baby on the face of this planet. You were pure joy. You made everyone around you happy. You made our family happy. You made the world happy and full of hope. You spent your days dancing and giggling and clapping your hands. You'd look at me and hold my face and say, "Mama, Mama, Mama." It's been so hard to live without you. I want nothing to do with a life without you. I miss you now, because on Saturday you would have turned three, but I also miss you as a five-year-old and a teenager, and I'm sad I won't get to see the man you would have become. You would have been all that is good and true in this world.

I don't know where you are. I want you back. You are my heart, and I'll live each and every day and each and every moment remembering you and living with my Ravi heart and taking care of your brothers and sisters. Thank you for teaching me the best kind of love that exists. Thank you for loving me more than I've ever been loved by anyone. Thank you for guiding me and protecting me these last few months as my guardian angel. The only thing worse than losing you would have been to have never loved you at all.

Love,
Mama

Before his departure, Jeremy calls a family meeting with the kids and asks them if he can marry me. Sitting downstairs, drinking my chai while the "mystery meeting" happens, I hear the kids burst out in happy cheers, shaking the house.

I go down to the office one morning and find Tope looking worried on the phone.

"How old are the girls?" he says flatly into the receiver. "Okay, we will discuss and make a plan to get out there."

"What happened?" I demand, sliding into the chair on the other side of his desk.

"There was a murder a few hours east of here." He sighs. "The father killed the mother with a machete. They have two little girls. They're referring the case to us."

My mouth turns rancid. After years of violence, I still don't have the stomach for it.

"How old?" I ask.

"Young. Nine months, and two years. They're from one of the forest tribes." Tope drops his head into his hands. "We can drive out tomorrow and look into it."

Even after living through a civil war and a career caring for orphans and refugees, Tope doesn't have the stomach for violence either.

At noon the next day, after a morning of contractor meetings, we hit the road in Tope's truck, twisting and turning for hours along the edge of the river, dipping into gullies and climbing out over steep, dust-covered hills. The sky darkens as we approach the village, a collection of shanties and homes cobbled together with mud and corrugated steel. The village head is waiting for us.

"Namaste," he says to me. His breath smells like alcohol, and his eyes are yellow.

"Namaste." I bow back to him.

I wander as I always do in these places, leaving Tope, who is infinitely more collected than I am, to gather information and documents. He's better on the ground than I am—less reactive, more empathetic, and also Nepali, which is critical. We're not interested in saving these communities—we're interested in empowering them. And as passionate as I am, Tope is the best person to do that.

Long-haired goats with matted beards chew their cud and nurse their babies as I walk by. There are girls marked with tikka, married way too young, and skinny little boys with sandy orange hair, maybe from malnourishment. A few men stumble around and stare expressionlessly at me, without either fear or curiosity, and usher their wives inside.

The small regional police building is several miles up the road and almost indistinguishable from other mud homes. An officer waits outside with a stack of papers and waves us inside. In Nepal, when parents go to jail, children often go with them. There are no social services. I head inside and see the babies, huddled together in a holding cell.

Two pairs of enormous brown eyes look up at me.

"Sisters," the officer says to me. I smile, thinking for a moment of Kate and Libby.

The littlest one is as fat as a koala bear, clearly breastfed. With a furrowed brow, she shakes a dirty canister of buffalo milk at me, not sure how to drink from it. The two-year-old smiles shyly, as though she's apologizing for her sister. Tope comes up behind me and waves at them. Nobody is better with babies than he is.

"Are there any relatives?" I ask.

"No grandparents," Tope says. "The mom had a sister, but she's young and has a lot of kids of her own. If there are others, they are most likely migrant workers in India. It could take us months to track them down, and if they're from this community, there is no way they could take on two more kids."

"What's the sentence for the father?" I ask, even though I know I don't want the answer.

"Twenty-five years. The police caught him while he was trying to get away. The girls saw everything." He clears his throat, which sounds hoarse and sick with the words that come from it.

He looks down at his paperwork and points to the baby.

"This is Khushi. It means 'happy.'" He grins, and Khushi bats her eyes at him.

"This is Khushbu." He motions toward the older girl.

"What does that mean?" I ask.

"'Smells good.'" Tope smiles.

Khushbu giggles, too, at the sound of her own name.

Ravi means "sunshine." I almost say it out loud.

Khushi lifts her arms to me. Her tongue pokes out from between her lips when she smiles, just like Ravi's did. My hands feel like hot glue, but she stretches her fingers up at me again and grunts. I wrap her in a rag and lift her, even though so much of me doesn't want to. The familiar weight settles on my chest. It knocks the wind from me. She nestles her head into the side of my neck, and slowly, we rock side to side. I'm not sure the house is ready for another baby and a toddler at the moment, but they have nowhere else to go.

Tope and I drive back to the village, through mustard fields and past dry husks of corn, to pick up the final documents. I duck into the girls' one-room hut to grab any photos or information, any toys or scraps of blanket that might comfort them. Their mother's blood is still smeared into the earth and onto the walls. I mourn for them, for all of my motherless children.

The village leadership and the police hand over custody on the spot. We drive for hours in the pitch dark toward Surkhet, and the girls sleep soundly across my arms, bodies warm and lips fluttering. I start to drift away with them. As the last slips of light fade from my eyes, a thought wanders casually into my mind.

My period is five days late.

Life rushes in and it rushes out.

16

A LONG SHADOW

_____

Dear Big N,
I believe in miracles. We were meant to find each other and
build this family of ours together.

—M

T HE LAKE WATER is cold in September, but it cradles my body
gently, lifting the weight of my belly and rocking it, just
slightly, back and forth. Everything is quiet. Neon canoes slip
silently onto the water's surface from the shore and drift off to
become colorless leaf shapes on the horizon. The wind is breath
from the deepest sleep. Like most days, I struggle to love the water.
The lake hoists my middle up with its strange liquid brawn until
only my big toes kiss the slick bottom of the basin. Karma, our
oldest in the home, is next to me, peaceful and still as she always is.

"Maggie Mom!"

The rest of the girls are cavorting in the shallows, calling my
name and waving from the khaki-colored beach, bright plastic
pails and frilly swimsuits full of sand. Breathing deep, I wave back
and rest a hand on my stomach, picturing the tiny lips, fingers,
and toes. At four months, the baby probably looks more like a
cuttlefish than a human.

Karma reaches out for my hand. "Don't worry—everything is
going to be okay," she assures me.

Even though it's early, I swear the baby twitches inside me, as if to say, "*She's right, you know. All I ever do is float. I'm safe here; so are you.*"

At first, I was afraid I wouldn't be able to love the baby as much as I loved Ravi. What scares me most now is that I will.

Tomorrow, Jeremy and I are getting married on a mountaintop. We decided to keep it simple, make it a celebration about the kids. We all loaded up and drove to Pokhara, a glacial lake the kind of shocking blue I normally only see on sports drinks and bird eggs. Some of Jeremy's family flew in from Canada to be with us. Mine will attend an eventual ceremony in the US, which we haven't started planning yet. His blond-haired nieces are impossible not to spot on the beach against the deep greens left behind by the monsoon. They chase Pabitra back and forth along the beach, and bursts of laughter travel to me like wind chimes. My muscles soften, and everything is right.

Thank you, thank you, thank you. I send my gratitude out toward the mountain and the sky.

———

THE GIRLS SPEND the night in my hotel room doing henna and pastel-colored, peel-off face masks that get stuck to our hairlines. The boys are with Jeremy, probably fast asleep from a day adventuring on the lake. Maya paints her nails a shiny pink and holds her henna-covered hands next to mine, comparing the curls and petals that climb up my wrist to those on hers. The room smells like fresh clove and acetone as we lay out our clothing and line up our shoes. We soak in the last moments of our family as it is and ready ourselves for what it will be.

Before we say goodnight, Jeremy's mom and the aunties sit us all in a circle. The girls, all of them, ages four through eighteen, want to share their womanly wisdom with me.

"Learn to make dal bhat."

"Be kind."

"Don't go to bed angry."

"Have lots of babies."

They give me sleepy kisses and head for their own hotel rooms. Because I can't help myself, I sneak down a floor to tuck the boys in.

"You know, we're pretty lucky. Not many kids get to go to their mom's wedding!" Krishna smiles as I turn off the lights.

"It's your last night as a single woman." Narendra laughs. He raises his fourteen-year-old eyebrows, all *hubba-hubba*.

"I love you," I tell him.

"I love you more!" he calls back to me.

"But I love you the most."

It's a battle he's let me win since he was five years old, but I'm not so sure I'm the victor. He loves me enough to let in someone new. He trusts me enough to know that when everything in life changes, nothing in love will.

BUSES COME FOR US around noon the next day, right when the sun comes out from behind a cottony Himalayan cloud. The little girls are wearing the matching dresses they picked out: gold sequins on top, shiny purple ribbon in the middle, giant white skirts flaring out to the knees. The older girls are in saris that shimmer whenever they step into the light, and the boys are decked out in traditional *daura saruwal*, long, closed-neck shirts, navy top coats, and *dhaka topi*, a boxy printed hat. Beyond yetis and Everest, the dhaka topi seems to be what Nepal is most famous for in the West. Jeremy is in daura saruwal, too, but his is gold and embossed with peepal trees shaped like spades from a deck of playing cards. In most Hindu ceremonies, the bride wears red, symbolic of, among other things, purity. The poppy-colored fabric groans across my pregnant belly when I climb onto the bus, which everyone except the priest seems to think is hilarious. Goma clears her throat and sings, "Going to the *stupa*, and we're gonna get married," as we drive *up*, *up*, *up* to the peak and stare out the open window into the crevices of the Annapurna range. Annapurna is the goddess of nourishment, and nourished is exactly how I feel: full, complete, protected by an infinite love.

The buses stop, and our family of seventy follows a skinny dirt path on foot up to an ivory stupa on the summit. From a distance, the little relic is a sleeping white whale against an ocean of rock. As we get higher, the path becomes more of an aisle, flanked by marigold tops and twinkle lights that guide us onward to the altar at the top. Jeremy and I sit next to each other under the *mandap*, which is made from four sturdy banana trees and a red blanket. Our children and friends gather around us, and the priest prays in a soothing, velvety monotone.

We wanted a ceremony that would honor the children and their culture. Most of them have never been to a wedding before, and when I steal a look, their faces are a mix of exhilaration, sobriety, and a desire to run off and chase the fat ground birds that waddle around the venue.

I wonder what I look like. I don't feel nervous, but my henna-covered hands and red painted nails are shaking. I'm eight thousand miles from Mendham, New Jersey, and everything I thought this day would be.

The rites are a swirl of light, color, and sacredness, some of which I can absorb and commit to memory. Others fly by like songs from a passing car's window, barely grazing my consciousness. The priest performs a pooja and leads us like a pair of lambs through the rituals: walking around the four banana trees seven times, sharing an apple, talking about our commitment, and resting our hands on one another's heart. By the end, I've acquired about seventy-five necklaces—some made of glass beads, others of flowers, and one *dubo ko malla*, a garland made of special grass chosen because it can grow without roots. My hair and face are covered in vermillion powder that Jeremy painted onto me to signify that I'm a married woman, and I'm so happy, vermillion tears drop from my cheeks. We exchange rings, and the kids go totally wild. Everyone hoots and hollers and lights orange lanterns that float up into the sky and toward the gray mountains. Tope goes wild, too, in a way I've never seen before, which makes me smile.

After a break to eat momos, take pictures, and play games, there's a short Western ceremony, which we only do so that we can read the vows we wrote and let the little girls sprinkle yellow petals, as they've seen on TV. With Karma on one arm and Keshav on the other, eight flower girls in front and the rest behind, all fifty-three kids walk me down the aisle. I drink them in like sugar water as they break away to find their seats.

Dear Madan,
You are my Dreamer.

Dear Rupa,
You make everyone around you feel loved.

Dear Man Kumari,
You are unstoppable.

The light changes as I walk on alone, and magnificent Annapurna drapes a long shadow over everything below, a darkness more vast and disarming than the elevation itself. I always believed that darkness and grief were what my children carried with them when they first lay their heads down at Kopila Valley. I understand now that it was love. Grief doesn't arrive because love is gone—it arrives because love is everywhere, because it's extraordinary, a mammoth that touches the sky. It stands not in opposition to love, but as a consequence of it. Grief is the shadow cast by the world's greatest wonder. When it falls, all we can do in our suffering is keep looking up for the light to change, for the miracle to reveal itself again. Just as I arrive by Jeremy's side, it does.

We blubber through our vows, and the children blow iridescent bubbles that pop on our cheeks. The sun sets orange on Annapurna, and we dance until it's time to go home as a family.

———

THE MONTH THAT follows is school construction, marital bliss, and wicked heartburn. In pregnancy, my body is a stranger to me. Jeremy thinks I'm beautiful, but the kids think I look like a snowman. I get winded when I speak during meetings. My boobs throb, and my toes swell themselves into cocktail weenies. Everything that I *know* tastes good tastes like white vinegar, and I hate Pacific salmon so much that one particularly embarrassing afternoon, I cry and gag just from the thought of it. For the record, there is no danger of a Pacific salmon fillet finding me anywhere in midwestern Nepal.

Every morning, driven more by discipline than hunger, I eat greens and pomegranate and take an iron supplement as big as an ice cube. All I really want is Ben & Jerry's Half-Baked and a vat of nacho cheese from Yankee Stadium, but I micromanage my pregnancy like it's another important project that has to be right. I add an obstetrician in Surkhet to my emergency contacts, and then two more OBs from the States, in case whoever is tending to me in the midst of a possible health crisis wants a second opinion, then a third.

When the kids go to school, I light a candle in my room and do birthing meditations that are supposed to calm me down.

> *I am safe; my baby is safe.*
> *My pelvis opens wide for my baby to pass through.*
> *I push all fear aside. I push all doubt aside.*

But I can't push all fear aside. It's a chatty bird that sits on my shoulder.

In Surkhet, women have babies without fanfare. They labor in the mud huts they built with their own hands, the rice paddies where they work, the forests where they gather firewood. Birth is as natural and inevitable as death, untouchable by the plans and wishes we make. Most women here don't even have a doctor. I have an app on my phone to alert me when my baby has grown from an ear of corn to a rutabaga. After I birth our baby, I'll drink bone broth and let my body rest. After my neighbor has hers, she'll isolate in a shed for chhaupadi until her body stops bleeding. I can't help but compare myself. I can't help but confront and shrink from my own privilege. Especially when Jeremy brings up having the baby in America. Up until 2000, Nepal was the number one country in the world for maternal and neonatal death. Having our baby here scares him, and though I'll never admit it, it scares me too. I don't know who I'll be if I leave my children again, if I choose to access care totally unreachable to any other woman in my community, including my own daughters.

Jeremy and I are both working in New York when it's time for my five-month checkup. Minus the fact that my esophagus feels like it's filled with Tabasco sauce, everything seems to be going fine. But it isn't. The doctor says my thyroid isn't functioning. One of my legs is bigger than the other. I'm gaining too much weight too fast, even though all I eat is lentils and rice. They admit me to the hospital for a litany of ultrasound scans and blood-sugar tests. Both of us are terrified, but only Jeremy has the courage to say so.

"What if we just stayed here?" he ventures.

"Maybe," I whisper, pretending to fall asleep so we don't have to talk about it.

For months, I'd dreamed about having all the other children by my side to welcome their baby brother or sister. I'd labor at home with the windows open and have Karma, who wants to be a nurse, time the contractions and slip ice chips under my tongue. The little ones would complain that it was taking too long and lose interest. The middles would shell Jeremy with questions about how the baby got there in the first place, and he'd sweat more than I would. Shivering, pink, and screaming, the baby would come—a girl, I think—and the midwife would place her body on mine to warm. She would rest on my chest for days, like she'd never known anywhere else, sleeping through a constant inventory of fingers and toes, through the sounds of brothers and sisters playing outside, through satsung at night and the chaos of morning. I would heal at home with Bauju's chai and goat stew, and the biggest love I've known.

After two days at the hospital, they discharge me, and against everyone's wishes, we go back to Nepal.

AROUND SIX MONTHS, I begin flashing back to Ravi. I waddle through the house on a tour of memories, reliving his first steps, the day he tried noodles, the first tooth, a white pebble poking through his gums, the day that he died. The afternoon is a reel that plays again and again.

I run downstairs.

I grab the CPR mask.

Ravi is wet and limp.

Padam is shaking.

I scream, a sound I could never re-create but will always feel in my throat.

After an episode, I'm not myself. I'm not anyone at all. I break a sweat brushing my teeth, and sleep becomes a joke. People have to tell me things four or five times before the words bust through the grief and sink in. The baby inside me stays up with me until 2:00 a.m. most nights, strumming my rib cage like a harp and reminding me how soon they'll be here. I thought I was ready, but I'm not.

"We need to go home. It's time to book our flights," Jeremy says to me, as we both lie sleepless in our bed, which is wet and sour from my hot flashes.

"We are home." I try to give his hand a squeeze, but my fingers are shaking. "I can have a perfectly safe delivery here. Kathmandu is filled with amazing doctors. Women have been doing this for thousands of years."

"Maggie, what if something goes wrong? Think of the baby."

He places a hand on my ribs. A little foot shifts and presses against his palm.

Think of the baby.

When I think of the baby, I still think of Ravi.

"I promise—everything will be fine." My voice trembles, along with the rest of me. We both know there's only one way I can be convinced to go.

————

"HOW CAN I leave? Don't you want to see the baby?"

I'm thirty weeks along when the children ambush me at satsung with a surprise baby intervention.

"There are too many viruses here, Mom."

"Somebody is always sick."

"You won't get any rest here."

"Babies are boring."

"You'll get to go to *California*!"

They all have reasons that they present to me. They want me to be safe and close to my parents; they want Jeremy to be able to see his dog, Bear; and according to Yagay, "*California*!" is reason enough on its own. I also get the sense from their pleading eyes and shifty, nervous bodies that there are other reasons they keep to themselves.

What if you get sick?

What if the baby dies like Ravi?

What if we lose you again just like we did last time?

It never even occurred to me that they could be as scared as I am.

I sift through a decade of life as I stare out into the corners of the green room, where we gather each day to sing and dance. Their faces are somber, filled with concern and love, wanting to care for me with the same desperation I wanted to care for them all those years ago and every single day since. I've made many mistakes in raising them, in trying to make a life here. I know I'll make many, many more. The only thing I've ever known for sure to be right has been listening to my children.

"Are you sure?"

Fifty-three heads bob up and down. That night, I book my plane ticket and sleep soundly for the first time in months.

———

AT THIRTY-FOUR WEEKS exactly, when the app says my baby is the size of a cabbage, but it feels like it's the size of a jackfruit, I put on my thickest, fuzziest sweater, gather my paperwork, and get ready to say goodbye to Kopila Valley, not knowing for sure when I'll be back.

The kids meet me in the side yard and take turns kissing my cheeks and patting my belly for luck. Maya places her hands on the ripples where my skin has stretched and whispers something to the baby that she refuses to tell me when I ask. Coyly, she shakes her head and grins like a fox. I hold on to each of the children as long as they'll let me. I hold on to all of it—the mountains, the home we built together, the smell of mustard oil and bitter greens from the kitchen that I normally hate but love like a friend today.

"Everything will be fine." Tope smiles, playfully shooing me away.

And I know it will be. Kopila and BlinkNow are surrounded and embraced by some of the best humans on Planet Earth. Sachyam, Aakriti, and the aunties are the best caregivers I could have ever wished for. Sachyam's big round eyes, framed by a thick curtain of lashes, almost seem to have a light behind them. He speaks with the calm, soothing voice of a guru and still giggles like a child. He has a body made for hugging and is the best big brother any child on earth could ever dream of. He breaks out loudly into Hindu devotional songs seemingly out of nowhere. He is everywhere at once, driving a child for a doctor's appointment one second and whipping up the best chicken tikka masala for sixty of us the next. He can somehow accomplish hundreds of tasks a day and keep all of our cylinders spinning.

Aakriti recently shaved her head and looks like a Buddhist nun straight out of a monastery. She has one of the most gorgeous faces I've ever seen, and yet is completely devoid of vanity. She's always wrapped in a warm, cozy sweater or shawl and carries herself with a gentle smile. She is kind, quiet, and often goes unnoticed because she is behind the scenes, taking the time to be present with each and every child. She is a gifted listener tuning in to hear all of what is spoken and also what is unsaid. She's a born caretaker who spends her time reading bedtime stories, doing tuck-ins, combing hair into perfect braids, calming worries, and organizing meal schedules and yoga rooftop sessions. Aakriti is always up for spontaneous rooftop dance parties in the rain or a quiet reading session in the sun. She's there by bedsides with soup and lemon tea for sick days and sleepless nights. I count my lucky stars for her every single day.

Naim and Jaddon run our school. Collectively, they have about fifty years' worth of experience in the education field and are committed to creating the best school in the entire world, with everything from teacher training to curriculum building to place-based and experiential learning techniques. Cal's handling day-to-day operations. He has the most perfect English accent that sounds like it's straight out of the Headspace meditation app. At first, he comes off as being super serious, but below the surface he is prone to deep, heart-to-heart conversations, debating conspiracy theories and astute observations. He is also capable of utterly silly jokes and fun Friday nights out with the team over cold gorkha beers at the roadside Gokhul shack across the street.

Luke is managing the construction of the new campus. He's a young and stunningly handsome shaggy-haired engineer from Vermont. I don't think I've ever met anyone so passionate about green building. Luke is actually passionate about everything in life, and when he's not working, he goes around planting passion fruit around the campus. Luke is on his fifth year with us, working all the hours that daylight offers on every inch of the school and often late into the night pouring through drawings and budget and construction management software. He's become a brother to me, an anchor and the point person for our Nepali construction, engineering, and architectural team.

Kelly and Rosna run the Women's Center. They show up at the police station for cases of assault and violence against women in the community. They run literacy classes, business training workshops, organize rallies, dispense microloans, and bring in a local female rights attorney to train our Kopila women on their human rights. The center has trained over 250 women in the making of beautiful shawls, school uniforms, tableware, bedsheets, warm pajamas for the kids, and so much more. The women at the center all care for each other deeply and have formed their own network of friendships and support. They take care of each other's children and support each other in their business endeavors. Rosna gets up and runs five miles every day before her long hours at the center, which she spends empowering and inspiring our women. She's sincere, strong, and kind. I know Rosna will go on eventually to graduate school and change the world, and it's been amazing to watch her bloom here.

Meelan directs the health and wellness programs and safe house. She has long dark glossy hair that blows behind her on her motorbike and big brown eyes that display her emotions. She is a feminist from Kathmandu who wears tomboy jeans one day and glamorous embroidered kurtas the next. The children all love her so much and are always flocking to her office. Meelan loves the kids just as her own and has become another mother figure to them. She sleeps with her phone next to her pillow and loses sleep at night thinking about our students, our safe home for girls, all of the emergency cases that have come our way that week. Meelan is an incredible leader of the counseling center, the health clinic, nutrition programs, family development and child safety and crisis intervention teams.

Jamie and his team run sustainability. He has brought in all the best minds on everything from wastewater management to rainwater harvesting, solar cooking systems, sustainable landscaping, and permaculture. He went with coconut husk for our soccer turf, and tries to ensure that every square inch of the campus is permeable. I barely see him because he's either up in a jackfruit tree, or working the compost pile, or in the dirt with the kids regenerating our soil with something carbon-fixing. There is nobody more principled than Jamie, especially when it comes to sustainability. He wears the same green T-shirt every day, mountain bikes to the site, and has committed his life here until this project is complete. He's my conscience who gives me a disapproving look when I buy juice boxes for the kids, our beloved role model and everyone's crush. He and Luke are on year five with us, speak near perfect Nepali, write in Devanagari script, and have unbending character, even with challenge after challenge when it seems there is no way we can finish this school.

Anjali and a committee of other international experts helped us launch Futures, a program to support our young adults and graduates during their transition into adulthood. There is no one who could have created this program better than Anjali. She thought through every last detail, consulting with organizations around the world and within Nepal that have gone through similar stages of growth. She built a curriculum and a checklist of life skills and workshops our students and home kids will need to be successful adults. She found college and university partnerships and scholarships and built a bridge between Kopila and various vocational skills and internship programs. She brought on Manjula and a team of guidance counselors to teach the kids everything from resume-writing to how to have a successful job interview and choose a career path. Everything she and the Futures team is doing is working!

We have both a strong local Nepali board and an amazing international one. Then there's Tope, who was born to lead all of them, our family of 120.

Everything I prayed for when we blessed this land and carved into it with our shovels has come to us. We haven't just grown; we've bloomed.

I sob the whole way to the airport, and before I can stop my tears, I'm crying again at the sight of two shimmering peaks out the plane window.

———

WE ARRIVE IN New Jersey to snow on the ground, hauling around the most pregnant belly the world has ever seen. (I actually have to assure people it's not twins.) The air is filled with holiday cheer. Christmas carols play in the supermarket and there are green wreaths everywhere I look. I do a few final speaking engagements to close out the year. It's also the ten-year anniversary of

BlinkNow, and our team, led by the one and only Kim Wentworth, beloved Eileen Quick, and dependable Ruth, has organized our first fundraising gala (but we insist on calling it a celebration!). They have planned this party for months, down to every last immaculate detail. They know me well, and instead of the usual black-tie event, we make it Nepali-themed, with color and decor and dance and music. They book an event space, and it's bursting with color and nearly 650 people. Everyone comes dressed in Nepali garb. We even find a celebrity host, and Billy Joel's band plays for us. Our BlinkNow supporters, our incredible board, my dearest childhood friends, our fellows, and the cast of characters that has shaped me and BlinkNow over the years, are all there in the room.

Maybe it's the fact that I'm thirty-seven weeks pregnant and about to burst, but as I stand on the stage at the podium and look out over a sea full of supporters and people who have stepped up for me and the kids through each and every stage of our growth, through each hardship and each joy, I can't help but sob. I see Tope front and center at a table with our entire international team and a few of our Kopila college students. I see my mom swallowing tears. I can see in her eyes how proud she is. I see Megan holding her heart and can almost hear her deep, raspy voice whispering, "You can do this, Mags." Her friendship, her hours of coaching and therapy, and the miles of long walks where she simply listened and kept me in check have carried me through all these years. I see Jim Duff, who we are honoring as "supporter of the year," beaming in his Nepali topi. He's poured every ounce of his heart and his life's earnings into our work, from land purchases to wings of the new campus. After he lost his wife, Beth, he was looking for a reason to keep going, and by some stroke of luck, he found us and we found him. Here he is, beaming in pride. I don't know where I'd be without him. I see my uncle Ed who has made six trips to Nepal and become my children's—and all of Nepal's—uncle Ed. I see all our board members from over the years. It's the most perfect evening. We raise enough money to finish our new dream green campus, and to support the kids and our programs into 2019. I can't believe it as I see the "text to give" numbers shoot through the roof on the big screens.

When it's my time to give a speech, I pull a joke together to stop the tears, hoping that my water won't break right then and there. I stand up and read a love letter. This time, it's to myself. All the things I would have told nineteen-year-old Maggie, all the things I would have told her that she never could have possibly known.

We dance into the most perfect night and end up in the lobby bar. I hug Kim and Eileen and Ruth, who are rocking saris better than anyone I've ever seen, and I'm tired and blown away by the night of success.

"I wouldn't be here without you," I tell them. And it's true.

At every twist, at every turn, there have been so many incredible people who have stepped up and were there by my side.

"Thank you. Thank you. Thank you."

JEREMY FINDS US an old Spanish-style house to rent in Altadena the day it comes on the market. He's in LA, finishing on set at a TV show until the day we are due. The birthing center is close by, and I can walk to the grocery store. We have friendly neighbors, and the sidewalks are made of concrete that's the same bright white as the stupa where we were married. The owners of our home are professors at Caltech, taking a residency at another college. They leave in a hurry and almost apologize for leaving the place fully and beautifully furnished, appointed with glassware, appliances, and half a jug of laundry detergent. Bear the dog moves in with us and spends his days patrolling the fenced-in yard, begging for food in the sunlit kitchen, and resting his head on my belly, until the baby kicks and he scuttles away from me, terrified.

While we wait for the baby, Jeremy works in the small studio out back, and Roda comes over to put a nursery together for us and to listen to me while I complain about the pressure in my uterus and rave about the icemaker in the refrigerator. I do all things "America" while I wait, like some kind of fanatical tourist. I order Postmates, sign up for Amazon Prime, take pictures of the Hollywood sign, and test drive a Tesla I can barely fit into in the hope it will induce labor.

My due date comes and goes.

At forty-two weeks on the nose, after good Mexican food and my first glass of wine in ten months, the contractions begin.

17

RUBY SUNSHINE

Dear H,
Everything you'll need is deep inside you.
—M

I feel calm.
I feel safe.
I feel secure.
I fully relax and turn my birthing over to my child.
My blood vessels close to the appropriate degree.

THE RUSHES COME on Nepali time, an early February evening two weeks later than they were supposed to. They begin
somewhere in the center of me and fan out over my body like a
sunburst, until I feel them as sputters from my lips and cramps in
the arches of my feet. Meditations drone on and on from Jeremy's
phone, as we sit in the bathroom and wait until it's time to go to
the birthing center, a moment we're told we'll recognize but have
never experienced. Light swells on the bathroom wall, and I watch
my shadow, more a gray landmass than a naked woman.

Jeremy has lit every single candle we own. They're perched on
odd ledges and recessed nooks in the wall, near the faucet and on
the back of the toilet (until my hair nearly catches on fire). He
places them around the water-filled tub as a glowing invitation.

I've been trying to get from the toilet to the warm water for an hour. If the baby arrives suddenly, we don't want the first thing she sees to be a plunger. I stand, shake, and stop. Stand, shake, and stop.

I put all fear aside and welcome my baby with happiness.
I turn my birthing over to my body.

The baby drops, and my lungs clamor for air, sucking in as much oxygen as they can, while they can. I nod at Jeremy, and he walks with me in a slow shuffle across the tile to the water.

I still hate the water, but my body is drawn to it. A bird's wings turn it south in October, a cow lies close to the ground before a storm, and my baby wants to be born in the water. Between surges, within surges, every part of me reaches toward the gentle sloshing of the bathtub. The *tato pokari*, as Juntara liked to call it, meaning "hot lake."

In this moment where I see nothing else clearly, I see her in technicolor. Smiling, laughing, playing. Telling me how strong she is. She wasn't supposed to die. Nobody was. Not Pampa or Manisha from school, who took her own life. Not babies in Jumla born to nothing or old people with everything in Los Angeles. Not Ravi. How do we keep living like this? Walking through the world a single step away from devastation. Why make our love so strong and our lives so fragile?

I turn my birthing over to my baby and to my body.

My back arches. A low groan hums through my lips. Birth feels as far beyond my control as death does.

Jeremy helps me slip one leg into the tub, then the other. The liquid curls silver around me, receiving me from him as a guest. I see Ravi now, perfect, fat belly, hands reaching for foamy tufts of bath soap, giggles reaching up to the sky. He loved the water too.

How can my baby's life begin where his life ended?

I imagine lifting her from the water, watching her ribs fan out and fill with life, listening to the very first sounds she makes. I see Ravi again, wet and empty, gone from the world.

Another surge comes.

I'm prepared to meet whatever turn my birthing might take.

But there is no preparing. Not for any of it.

———

AFTER THIRTY HOURS laboring at home, we drive to Good Samaritan Hospital, not "GraceFull Birthing," around ten o'clock at night. It's time to check on the baby, they said. For reasons I can't explain, I put on a pretty rust-colored dress with polka dots on it, the kind of thing you'd wear to a wedding or polo match. Jeremy wears his sweats. When we arrive, I lean over a waiting room chair and sway my hips back and forth under hot white tubes of fluorescent light, listening to an arcade of bleeping medical machines and call buttons. Jeremy checks us in and holds my hand steady through a contraction.

"We're not supposed to be here," I sob.

He stares into my eyes. Deep love. Deep, unwavering soulmate love. Mighty, forever love, the only thing we can promise each other in life. We wanted to do things differently. This isn't the set we designed, with the tub and the essential oils and the good lighting, but here we are, in a fluorescent hospital lobby in the middle of the night, together. Maybe this is exactly where we're meant to be.

———————

THE NAME "RUBY" hits me on the operating table under heavy sedation. When I was twelve or thirteen, my parents took me camping. We were staying in a primitive sort of cabin-thing, and a little girl named Ruby was staying in the cabin next to ours. I'd hear her mom yelling out for her: "Ruby! Ruby!" She was always playing outside. I got used to it, the way you do with forest sounds. A bird chirps, the wind blows, "Ruby! Ruby!"

That's a nice name, I remember thinking. *If I ever have a daughter, I'll name her Ruby.*

I kept it and locked it away somewhere deep in my heart, until now.

I'm calm from the drugs and staring up at the moon-shaped operating room lights. I think I might be smiling. A nice lady washes my body and prepares it for surgery. She wipes my belly with something that smells like isopropyl alcohol and shaves a spot near my hips, where the incision will be. Jeremy comes in, a lumbering blue giant. At first, I can't recognize him. He's got the same scrubs, hospital hat, and mask that all the nurses have. I only know that it's him when he looks into my eyes and speaks to me.

"I'm here. We get to meet our baby soon. Everything is going to be okay. I'm smiling under this mask, I swear."

The anesthesiologists make one final check, and a big, gauzy curtain rises up from my sternum.

I try to remember the birthing meditations:

I feel calm.
I feel safe.
I feel secure.

Then, through a fog of exhaustion, sedation, joy, and grief, love arrives.

Dear Ganga,
I hope you never stop playing, never stop laughing. Stay
bossy, stay strong.

Dear Krishna Shahi,
I want you to stay just the way you are, forever and ever.

"Don't worry if the baby doesn't cry right away when she comes out," somebody says.

Dear Krishna Bogati,
I love you more than words.

Dear Sundar,
You are a gift. You are my pride. You are small, but you are
mighty.

They handle my body like a package. "It'll be just a few minutes!"

Dear Santosh,
I'll love you until the end of time.

"Ohhh, the baby's face is up! It's a girl! She's a chunky monkey! What a head!"

My insides quake from the pressure.

Dear Janak,
You can do anything and be anything.

An angry, guttural cry comes as soon as her skin hits the air. The doctor lifts her for me to see. My daughter is long, shockingly pink with brown wisps of hair. She's also enormous. The scale in the corner says nine pounds, eleven ounces when they lay her on it. She screams and screams and screams, until my lips are on her cheeks and she's resting, still wet, on my chest, exactly where she belongs. Jeremy takes our new baby girl out of the operating room holding her skin to skin and promises me he'll stay with her. As soon as I'm stitched up and get to recovery, she nurses and we examine every little toe and finger. She looks startlingly similar to Jeremy and I gasp when I see a heart-shaped birthmark on the side of her thigh. I find my phone and snap a picture. We instant message the kids: "She's here! You have a baby sister."

———

RUBY IS RESTING with a boob in her mouth when a neonatologist and a parade of NICU nurses, who I've never seen before, come to take her. Her lips are a perfect pink accordion fold between her cheeks, and there's a little pool of breast milk on her chin. I don't understand what's happening. She's been with us less than a day.

"Your baby has an infection," the doctor says without a shred of emotion. "Her white blood cell count isn't where it's supposed to be. We need to treat her in the NICU and she needs a spinal tap right away."

Jeremy stands up from a dead sleep like the room is on fire, and I cradle Ruby closer into me, convinced they've got the wrong kid.

"No, she's fine! Look at her! She's so pink. She doesn't have a fever. She just passed her hearing tests. They came in this morning. Nothing is wrong with her!"

A timid, brown-haired nurse scoops her from my bare chest and places her in a clear plastic bassinet. They wheel her out of the room and into the elevator. She's gone before I formulate a thought. I let my daughter go.

"Jeremy!"

I prop myself up on the pillows and get ready to follow her, forgetting that I can't walk yet. My staples pull for the first time, and there's an awful yelp. I can't do anything to save my baby. I'm physically and emotionally cut open. My legs are heavy, dead things, and all I can do is reach feebly toward the door.

"Go with her," I tell Jeremy, my anchor, my steadiness, my crying heap of a husband on the edge of the bed. "Don't leave her no matter what."

He wipes his eyes, kisses me, and runs toward the elevator bank. Then I'm alone.

What if I lose her?

What if she doesn't come out of that NICU?

What if this infection kills her?

What if they can't treat it?

What if she gets a fever and then starts having seizures and then has a bleed in her brain and then they have to put a shunt in, and it fails?

What if I have to bury her?

*What if I have to hold a dead, limp, cold baby body in my
arms again?*

What if she stops breathing?

What if her heart stops?

I'll die. I'll die again.

I spin and spin, helped along by the hydrocodone they gave me
for the pain and the exhaustion, not just of the past seventy-two
hours but the past ten years. I grieve for Ravi, Juntara, and Manisha, all the women and children I hoped to help but didn't. I grieve
for Ruby, having failed her already. The gravity of motherhood hits
all at once and so do shame, fear, and regret.

I can't breathe.

I slam the call button with my fist.

"Please help me!"

A nurse comes. Her eyes are crystal blue and as wide and pan-
icked as mine are. We both watch, alarmed, as my chest heaves and
my body tries to throw up the nothing in my stomach.

She leads me to the toilet and holds me there for a long time,
while I cry and pee without feeling it. She wipes my eyes, my
cheeks, and everything else. She remains a nameless angel—my
sister, my mother, and Bauju rolled into one—rubbing my back,
changing my diaper, and showing me the fabled, otherworldly
nurse love I've been told about by other moms. She tucks me back
into the bed, and I let myself feel like a child for the first time
in over a decade. When Jeremy calls, she answers and holds the
phone to my ear so I can talk to him.

"I need you to stay calm," Jeremy says. "Ruby's here, and she's
okay. You can come up and see her. They just put an IV in. When
you get here, you need to stay calm. There are machines and some
really sick babies. I can come get you if you want me to."

"No, don't leave her. I'll be there. I'll be there soon. I need to see her."

But part of me, a large part, can't bear the idea.

We left Surkhet so that nothing bad would happen, but it happened anyway. My daughter is ill, suffering just like the stranger-babies that used to show up swaddled outside Kopila Valley. I'm in LA. I'm privileged. Even with a gash in my belly and a sick child, I have more good fortune than I could ever deserve. None of us, whether we're in a mountain village or the Hollywood Hills, is in control. None of us conducts the rhythms of life and loss. All we can do is move with them together, connected by our frailty, as gracefully as we can. Whether we know it or not, we're our strongest that way.

I look out the window and notice the smooth, white tops of the mountains—the San Gabriels, I think. For a moment, they're my mountains, the loving, green Himalayan foothills.

Our doula comes to wash my face with bar soap and help me brush my teeth. She picks the tangles from my hair and tucks my boobs back into the hospital gown. They leak onto her nice jeans, but she doesn't mind. Without saying a word, we walk together, slower than slow, toward the elevator. I shudder when I see the word *NICU* on the button to the eighth floor, and we begin to rise.

The doors open, and a bell rings. We turn left and begin to walk. I cling to the railing on the wall the way I clung to the side of Maha Bua at eighteen years old. Weak, frightened, feeling like a kid again, I climb my way to Ruby.

The room is everything I feared it would be, an orchestra pit filled with noisy machines plucked and strummed by tiny sleeping bodies in matching striped caps. The sounds of life and death blur into one another, and the light is gray, reminiscent of neither night nor day. Ravi was in the NICU for months. That hospital and this one couldn't be more different, but the feelings of the NICU are the same. The darkness. The fear. The looks in the other parents' eyes. Beeping machines and tangled wires. The knowledge that, at any moment, any of our children could slip away.

Ruby is easy to spot, a squishy piglet about four times the size of the other babies. Jeremy has decorated her isolette with Nepali prayer flags, and he's standing over her, watching her little arms and legs swim through the air. We wrap each other up in as much love and strength as we can find in a room where even the air feels small and stale.

"She'll be ready to eat soon." A nurse smiles, nodding at a soft blue recliner in the corner. I didn't know if I'd get to touch Ruby. I didn't know if I'd want to. Our doula helps me settle into the chair and leaves us. The nurse lays Ruby, who is just beginning to stir, on my chest, perfect pink lips searching and smacking. She has my eyes, Jeremy's brows, my chin, his nose, and somehow, a part of each one of my children. I feel them in her little rabbit heart, and I feel them in mine. I lift a large, swollen breast from under the gown, and she latches on.

"She's eating!" I cry. No one told me she wouldn't. It's all she knows how to do, but somehow it feels miraculous, her jaw churning and eyelids fluttering up and down in a blissful, drunken dream cloud. She's covered in so many wires it's like breastfeeding a Play-Station, but I don't care. Neither does she. We're together, right where we belong.

When Jeremy goes to call our parents and the room grows quiet, I tell my little girl all about home, her fifty-three brothers and sisters, the slow-moving river, and the mountains that will watch over her, just like they did me.

"You have a big brother named Ravi," I whisper to her as she begins to drift off. "His name means 'sunshine.'"

She grunts and nestles into me, one fragile little life leaning into another. All we can do, as life rushes in and rushes out, is hold each other close and let love shape us. Let it be what shapes the world.

———

THE DOCTORS NEVER find out what the infection is. They tell us it could have been a number of things. Maybe it was the fever I had in labor or the meconium? They had diagnosed her with some sort of white blood cell infection but weren't able to identify exactly what it was. It doesn't really matter. The medicine is working, and Ruby is getting stronger. We spend nine days in the NICU, laying her on our bare chests and bathing her in the sink. She loves the water. When it rushes over her skin, she mews like a kitten. Eight thousand miles away from Surkhet, we find home in the blue chair, the mechanical soundscape, and the gray lights that give us no hint of the time. I dream of morning chai and fresh papaya, the sounds of the river and satsung. I miss the children but, in some ways, I've never felt closer to them than I do right here, right now. Their love is with me, in me, a Mother delicately carved from solid rock by the joy and sorrow of fifty-four miraculous lives. It is the best thing I could ever hope to be.

In the shadow-filled room, suspended between life and death, we let ourselves fall in love, madly and with no restraint. We look for the light, and we find it. We see our Ruby, brilliant, chubby, and bright.

"What if we call her 'Ruby Sunshine'?" Jeremy asks the night before we leave.

"It's perfect," I whisper, careful not to wake her.

Dear Ruby Sunshine,
You have a massive head, long eyelashes, and furry eyebrows.
You have weirdly elegant hands and what Daddy calls "piano
fingers." I love you so much it takes my breath away. I can't
wait to take you home.

xoxox,
Mom

18

DEAR CHILDREN

Dear K,
When you slow down and stop by my side, I see your love
and innocence, your warmth and wonder.

— M

Ruby's reflection is faint and ghostly in the airplane window. The softness of her cheeks blends into the thick meadow of cloud. Her mouth is a crumpled bird-shape. She sleeps as the captain mumbles announcements over the speaker, and I reach underneath her warm body, only three months old, to buckle my seat belt. She sleeps as the plane dives and wobbles and is still sleeping when all is steady again. When she wakes, two peaks cut through the mist, snow-covered and glowing like moonstone. *Nepal.*

"We're home, Ruby." I press a finger to the cold, clear plastic. Her face is projected against the vista, a perfect little mountain spirit, and she falls into a deep sleep again.

Jeremy is beside us with his camera. He's been filming me since our first date and has been working on a documentary about Kopila Valley. He sneaks a shot of Ruby and the mountains and turns back to Nisha, my first daughter, who is sleeping in the seat behind us. We picked her up from college in Amsterdam, on our way to Nepal. Soon, she'll be in Senegal taking a gap year, just like I did.

DEAR CHILDREN

"Be careful," I tell her, only half-joking. "You might fall in love with the place and never come home."

Or maybe she'll find home.

I look back at her asleep in her seat, and she could be seven years old again; in an instant, she's a woman, then a child. The captain mumbles, and Ruby kicks her feet, slowly waking up to the world again.

The first three months of her life were simple and full of bliss. In LA, our biggest tasks of the day were to feed her, change her, and introduce her to good music. We hiked and strolled around the block. We ate cereal, frozen pizza, tuna fish, lasagna, and soup, lots and lots of soup. We even made a few friends in our neighborhood, which was filled with dogs and babies and was, save for the much better weather, not such a different street from the one I grew up on. A sweet little place for sweet little families.

Inevitably, at a barbeque or a farmer's market, with Ruby tucked into her carrier, snoozing, somebody would ask the question:

"Is this your first baby?"

I'd never know how to answer it. Sometimes I said, "First biological, but I have other children." Sometimes I'd just say no. Most people left it alone, but others pressed on.

"Where do they go to school? Pasadena? Altadena?"

"Nepal." I smile.

Now and then, even after that, I'd get, "Oh, where's that?"

Not that long ago, I didn't know where Nepal was either.

California gave us space and sunshine and fresh lemons from our tree, but the mountains were more gray than green. The lake wasn't Bulebule.

When Ruby's vaccinations were up to date, we visited with our friends and families and said goodbye.

The plane sinks lower. Ruby squirms in my arms, and her face scrunches from the pressure. I begin to nurse her like the pediatrician told me I should, and Jeremy rubs her foot, which is still as small as an orange segment. The wheels drop, a brown quilt of farmland appears, and with a thud, we're home.

―――――

WE PULL UP to Kopila Valley just as the school bus goes by. Our family is waiting. The little ones are in their uniforms of greens, blues, reds, yellows, and the older kids are in their street clothes. Some of them have moved out already. Bishal has a mustache, and Keshav and Krishna are nearly as tall as Jeremy. Baby Khushi is twice as big and joyful as I remember her. I see her perched on Aakriti's hip and clapping her hands. Tope and Sachyam are talking with their "business things" faces on and their hands on their hips, half-watching Himal dribble a soccer ball across the dry, brittle earth, his tongue twisted out of his mouth in concentration.

I see them before they see me, and I'm glad. I need a second to take it all in. I've missed absolutely everything: the giggles of the kids and the loose teeth, the doughy cheeks, countless hugs, and the sounds of at least eight kids reading aloud outside my window. I've missed my coffee and breakfast with the other directors, our evening satsung, chats around the fire, and Friday night movies. I've even missed the teenage drama, which is mostly about dyeing or cutting hair. I've missed walking around the new land and dreaming with Tope. The dreaming phase is over now.

I watch them for just a moment in what I know are the last bits of quiet, before they'll hold the baby and cover me with kisses, before the aunties will rub tikka on my forehead and place flowers around my neck, before we sing and dance and eat together. I've been gone for months; the youngest ones won't remember me. I'm no longer the primary caregiver. This home has never felt less like mine and more like theirs, a shift I knew would happen and should happen, but feels like a sudden and heavy *thunk* in the midst of the frothy lightness and joy.

The next generation of Nepali children that come to us at Kopila Valley will be raised by Nepali caregivers. They will live in an empowered Nepali community and learn in an exceptional Nepali school. I'll more likely be "Maggie Auntie" than "Maggie Mom." This is my home, but I'm also a guest here.

I realize now that I've been the face of the organization for so many years, and ridden the waves of press and praise and language like hero and savior, that it's time to quietly sit back. I realize that my story was elevated throughout the past decade in the press because of what I look like and where I'm from, while the stories of the Nepalis by my side and the change-makers and people of color working in their own communities are often not. Tope and I always wrote it off because we could leverage the story and turn it into change and direct action on the ground, but there is less and less of a need to do that now. The world is changing. We have evolved. As Maya Angelou suggests, "we know better and are trying to do better" when it comes to the way we tell our story. Our team on the ground, our graduates, and members of our community can speak for themselves.

We've become so much more than that story of the girl with the backpack and her babysitting money and the garage sale in New Jersey. We are more than that initial picture of me standing in the hole of the foundation of where our future home would be. No more hero language, no more competing against other incredible causes and nonprofits with online popularity votes. No more Mabelline makeovers or having my picture plastered all over Doritos bags. We are creating stronger boundaries around allowing news and media outlets to only publish my picture and my story when the piece comes out, and we are being more careful about the language we use in our communications. As people in positions of privilege and power, it is our responsibility to help, not constantly be the center of the story with awards and medals.

I will continue to use my whiteness as an ally, elevate the voices and the stories of those around me, and disrupt the extreme inequality we continue to see in our world, perpetuated by those in positions of power. I see it as my responsibility to pass the baton on to the next generation of world travelers, gap year students, and people who want to bring about change to do this work ethically and in deep community partnership and collaboration. That, in fact, is the only reason why our work has been successful and sustained itself throughout the years. We know more than we ever have before. There are right ways to travel, and there are wrong ways to travel. There is a way to do this work ethically and conscientiously and in partnership, and there are ways that create real and true harm. We now have blueprints to learn from and models for success, and I feel very fortunate that we've transformed our mistakes and learnings into making us a better and stronger blueprint for others to follow.

Reflecting on my own journey, one of the greatest gifts is just how young I was. I knew that I didn't have any of the answers and then was graced and surrounded by a team of people like Tope who had walked the walk and had plenty of solutions. What my youth and starting from scratch also gave us was the ability not to strive for perfection, to start small, start with what we had: our hands, an open heart, and a welcoming community who wanted to be right by our side. We also looked deeply where development failed and tried not to repeat the common mistakes. Sometimes, in trying to take action or make a difference, we can fall into the trap of wanting to do everything perfectly, and in doing so, we wait. We wait until we have more time on our hands, or the right career, or financial stability to give back. But there is no time to wait.

I know from having witnessed it all these years that this work is effective and education is the path to creating long-lasting change. It's baby steps, it's small actions that we take and decisions we make as a collective human family working together. Kopila and BlinkNow are what they are today because I was humbly welcomed and warmly embraced by an incredible local Nepali community. I was an outsider and very far from an expert, and they were forgiving of that. I was helpful in bringing outside resources in to do the work the community wanted to do for itself and I tried my hardest to listen and learn. I hope to be a part of this work for the rest of my life, and I will never stop learning. It is the only thing that has gotten me and us as an organization this far.

Nisha darts out in front of us. The brothers and sisters spot her and come toward us in a stampede, bringing so much sound and color that the street dogs hide and the birds fly from the branches of our skinny old tree. Arms and laughter come from all directions. Himal yells as mightily as he can, and Karma speaks softly, giving Ruby's belly a tickle and holding us in a big hug.

"Welcome home!" Tope says. He gives me a hug and lifts Ruby up to show her where the big green mountains are. Jeremy smiles at me, kids hanging from his arms and legs and neck. Love is extraordinary, and it is absolutely everywhere.

OVER THE NEXT year, Ruby and Khushi become best friends. Ruby watches Khushi toddle and crawl, and in the blink of an eye, she's doing the same. She speaks in the thick Nepali accent that Jeremy and I can only dream of mastering, and she puts away dal bhat with the best of them. She spends her days studying her brothers and sisters as they fly kites from the roof and read books under the papaya tree. She bounces on Tope's knee during our planning meetings and sneaks paper-thin slices of mango from the aunties, listening to the songs they sing and watching with wide eyes as they butcher chickens and goats. She likes to play peekaboo with me from behind the shimmering green mosquito net over our bed, just like Ravi used to do, and she thinks Jeremy is the best guitar player on the planet.

Of all things a baby can do, her very favorite is to look at herself. She'll grab the freaky funhouse mirror on the top of her baby play gym until she has it at just the right angle, and she'll sit and wait patiently for puddles left behind by the monsoon to grow still and silver. We all marvel over how many hours she can spend staring at herself, smiling, cooing, and gabbing away. I wonder often what it is that she sees in her reflection, whether she knows it's her or thinks it's an incredibly agreeable white friend who shows up from time to time. She doesn't look like her brothers and sisters. We're not sure if she knows that yet, but one day she will. In these first years of fleeting innocence, people are all the same, and color is meaningless; nobody has more or less than anyone else. Hunger is a problem solved with a single cry, and despair is just a silly face away from rapture.

With her great big blue-gray eyes, blond hair, and American passport, Ruby's life will look different than the lives of the children she's growing up with, even though they'll go to the same school, sleep in the same bed, and eat the same food. Our world will value Ruby differently and afford her, as it does me, more privilege. The same legacy of colonialism and inequality that haunts her brothers and sisters in life will protect her. She'll have every opportunity to make a difference or not to. I'm not sure how she'll juggle that. I can only hope that as she takes her first steps in Surkhet, says her first words in Nepali, and makes her first friendships and memories here, she'll feel the same sense of home, family, and connectedness that I do, which she'll carry wherever she goes. I hope that she'll use her privilege. I started at eighteen, and I believe now that it was too late to begin.

———

AFTER SIX YEARS of grueling construction, planning, building, and one impossible barrier after the next, our new green campus is ready in February 2019. Friends and families and foundations with big hearts from all around the world have made it happen. It rains for days before our opening ceremony. We have an enormous celebration, filled with magic and meaning and color, dancing and tear-soaked speeches and incredible love. Our Surkhet community shows up to honor us, packing the courtyard until the soft, jade-colored grass is invisible. This school will belong to this small city long after Tope and I are gone. Blessing this land, this school, without them would be impossible. This is where their children and their great-great-great-grandchildren will learn.

Our BlinkNow team, board members, and dearest friends and supporters from Nepal and around the world arrive, minus my father, who passed away suddenly in the summertime. Like Ravi, I feel him with me often, but especially here, especially today. *This* is why he agreed to wire his eighteen-year-old daughter her five thousand dollars to start a life, all alone, in Nepal. I could never have imagined a wonderland like this one back then, but maybe he did. Maybe he saw all of it. I remember thinking that nothing could grow from the pale, waterless earth here, but everything did.

The campus is breathtaking. All the buildings are made from rammed earth, and it's solar powered and sustainable through and through. The rain we harvest from the monsoon will go through a purification system and last us all year. Our wastewater will be recycled, used again and again. We have a farm with cows, chickens, and goats, rows and rows of fresh, organic vegetables, and orchards filled with fruit. We have a place to grow mushrooms and potatoes, which, after years of learning and teasing, I'm now becoming an expert at. Kids play in each and every corner in outdoor classrooms, green spaces, and beautifully lit indoor spaces with big airy windows looking out onto the local forest, the old ancient temple, the beautiful bodhi tree, the mountains and the sky. There's room to expand and grow and accommodate the future children that will inevitably come our way. We see a future of exporting our model, and open sourcing our programs, and all of our learnings over the years to come. Over four hundred students are enrolled, and we employ over one hundred Nepali staff members across our many programs that are strong and robust and deeply rooted in community development and creating generational change. Kopila Valley is Nepal's greenest school, and everywhere I look, I see flashes of green, reminders of growth, joy, and healing. I hope our students, whether they are daughters of the mountains or sons of the Brahmin, can see them too.

Jeremy and Ruby wave to me from the front row, and I get ready to speak. The sun pours down on our school, sheathing it in light, a gem as precious as Odanoku. I walk toward the podium, strangely nervous after years of standing behind them and talking, and look out at all the people. I see my husband—my soul mate, the best man in the entire world, the one who never stole my heart but restored it with gentleness and unwavering love. I see my baby daughter, who one day will play soccer on the soft turf here, learn in the classrooms, and find shade under the thatched-roof gazebos. I see Tope—my brother, my mentor, my leader. The orphan boy who dropped out of school at age eleven to care for his family; who at thirteen traveled to India to be a child porter; who managed to get an education and a job; who decided, successful and happy, to go back to Nepal to help others and trusted me to do it with him. I see my Kopilas, all fifty-something of them, some just out of diapers and others in college. Our graduates all come back for the ceremony and I see them looking around the new campus proudly and telling the younger generation of students just how lucky they are. They are in universities, vocational programs, internships, and jobs all around the world. They are becoming educators, medical workers, engineers, scientists, farmers, and business owners.

And I see Hima—the little girl in orange from the riverbank, my first true glimpse of the world in all its grief and all its hope, the child who changed everything. She grins at me, eyes beaming like they were the day we met. She's in her final year of high school at Kopila and will soak in the new campus this year before she graduates.

I tell Tope's story, which isn't told nearly enough, and I tell ours, which everyone in the audience is a part of. I try to say thank you, but there are no words that are beautiful, meaningful, or joyful enough. Our school song, "We Are the Kopilas Blooming Every Day," plays, and we all cry and cheer and clap together. The mountains seem to hold us closer as the afternoon sun dips down to meet them. I step off the stage, and the kids who shaped me gather around to dance. As our bodies move together, I write one last letter, not to my children, but to *our* children.

Dear Children,

I dream of a world where your childhood is preserved, where you're not forced to grow up too soon, where you can laugh and play and skip all day. I see kites and swings and marbles and endless games of hide-and-seek for you.

I dream of healthy food for you to grow, vegetables for you to harvest, and fruit growing on trees for you to pick and toss down.

I dream of a world without violence, without the army marching on the streets with weapons every day. Where your vote matters, and you use it to vote for a candidate who believes in peace. I dream of a world where you can be that candidate.

I dream of a world where you can marry who you want, when you want to.

I dream of a world where you can make mistakes. As long as you are learning, you are living. Don't stop learning.

I dream of a world that cares for its weak, its sick, its handicapped, its widowed, its orphaned, its vulnerable. And a world where love rules. Love of all kinds.

xoxox,
Maggie

With love, the world can change in the blink of an eye.

Epilogue
SATSUNG

A T THE END of the day, the sky in Surkhet holds nothing
back. The mist fades by midmorning, and all afternoon, a
part of me is waiting for the moment that the air cools, when the
first of the crickets and the last of the birds sing the same song.
The outside voices that shout in the garden begin to quiet, long-
ing to be brought in for rest. Kites dive down to collide with the
roof one final time, and jump ropes are abandoned, left curled up
like snakes in the grass. One star appears in the deep blue. Then
another.

Like morning, evening at Kopila Valley is a frenzy. Teenagers
come home from soccer practice with aching muscles and sour-
smelling shoes. Middle kids wrestle with the last bits of homework, and little ones are surly and tired. We eat dinner, normally
rice and lentils but sometimes chicken or goat, and afterward, in
the midst of the wildness, of sixty lives in one house, we lay down
our good books and games to find peace, carving out a space in
the day for satsung.

Satsung is my favorite time of the day. It means "the company
of true people" in Sanskrit, and when we gather upstairs in the
green room facing each other, I feel a singular truth alive in me:

I'm home. I'm doing what I'm meant to do with my life, in exactly the right place with the exact right people. Our satsung is usually part meditation, part family meeting, part dance battle. We sing songs like "Resham Firiri," a popular folk ditty that everyone loves but nobody seems to understand, or something silly from my childhood like "Four Green and Speckled Frogs." The teenagers are somehow still completely into satsung, and get us all going with their wild clapping, chanting, off-the-hook dancing, and occasional backflips. We all sit in a pile on the floor, cuddled in blankets and each other. It will never get old, and it will always be our favorite part of the day as a family.

Usually I begin our time together with "requests," which are simple housekeeping matters:

"Remember, we always put water in the toilet after we use it."

"Remember when you have a book, you have to be gentle and not rip pages out."

Then we do "compliments," an opportunity for one person to celebrate another. Pabitra had an incredible report card. Deepak did a really good job with dinner duty tonight. That chicken was so good. After that, we talk about the next day, whether anything special or different will be happening. Like all children, ours like to know what to expect, and they thrive on a schedule. Lately, none of us has been able to predict what tomorrow will look like.

In January 2020, Nepal reported its first case of coronavirus. Lockdowns began in India, forcing a massive reverse migration of displaced Nepali laborers that continues today, over a year later. Some walked hundreds of miles from the brickyards or sorghum fields they worked to one of twenty border crossings, and then they journeyed hundreds of miles beyond them to the remote villages they left. Migrant camps have sprouted up quickly by the border and along the main roads. Thousands of men, women, and children travel without food or water and are forced to sleep together at the side of the road in the middle of a pandemic. We mobilized early on, securing donations of food and water, testing kits, and personal protective equipment (PPE). Like the rest of humanity, we didn't know how bad things would get, but the world changed, as it does, in the blink of an eye. We continue to do our best to change with it.

At the time of this writing, it's summer, and we've been quarantined for weeks at home. Our in-person programming is suspended. The Women's Center and Kopila Valley schools are temporarily operating remotely. The young adults are home from college, quarantined in an apartment across the road from us. At least two of them have tested positive already. Ruby and Jeremy were evacuated by the British embassy and are in Canada with his parents, a decision we normally would have wrestled with for weeks but which we made in a matter of hours. I miss them so much, it brings me to my knees.

The power goes out in long stretches every day, and the police patrol our streets in their jeeps, shouting over the loudspeaker for residents to stay inside. With a fragile healthcare system, arguably in a state of crisis already, lockdowns are the best possible hope of avoiding catastrophe. Still, women and children show up at our gates every day, with nothing to eat and no other place to go. All work for daily wage laborers has halted, and families are going for weeks without a single wage. We send them on to our food bank and do our best to support them as safely as possible.

My biggest concern, as always, is for the children. Not just our Kopila children, but the world's. And the only way to keep all children safe is to work together, to gather as the human family I know in my bones that we are.

In our tall yellow house in the Surkhet Valley, the kids are safe and happy. Instead of mourning, they've been spending their days sorting food donations, organizing workbooks and educational materials for their classmates, and loading our bus with cases of water and masks sewn by the women in our cooperative. In this moment, they choose to move together, work together, and give whatever it is they can to a world that long ago stole everything and everyone they loved. They're survivors of cruelty and injustice, unimaginable disasters just like this one.

One day, they may share their stories with the world, write their own books, or give their own TED Talks. They may never find the words, or they may never want to. Life rushes in and it rushes out, but what they leave in their wake at the end of these long, strange days says everything about who they are, and in this unimaginable reality, who we all can be. They are a perpetual reminder to me of the choices we can all make right now, especially those of us in positions of privilege. We can choose love. We can let it be what shapes us and serves as the bedrock of a new world. We can create the world we want to live in, and the first step is believing that it's possible.

Night after night, in this uncertain world, we continue to meet in the satsung room and rejoice in the truth we find here. There is much to be grateful for, and there is much we can give. Sachyam, who has been driving to the quarantine camps and food stations all day, turns on the music, the latest Bollywood hit. Pabitra stands up first, Maya shoots up right after, and one by one, we all follow and begin to dance. We move best when we move together. We are one human family. There isn't another second to waste.

Acknowledgments

─────────────

To my kopila children. As you continue to grow up and create your own stories, I want you to have mine, as a reminder of my love for you and our lives together.

To Ravi. I love you. I'm so sorry. Your loss still feels impossible. I miss you every moment of every day. I carry your heart in my heart.

To our team and our board members at BlinkNow and Kopila. Thank you for being a part of the vision and for the incredibly hard work you put in each day to make our little corner of Nepal and the world a place where every child is safe, educated, and loved. I couldn't ask for a better team. Tope, Kusum, Daju, Bauju, Sachyam, Aakriti, Basanti, Shangkar, Manju, Amrika, and Sukma, thank you for being on this journey and parenting with me each and every step of the way. Tope, thank you for being our cofounder and always knowingly guiding the way. Your partnership is without a doubt what has made our organization what it is today. To the teachers, social workers, mentors, and Nepali community, and leadership team we have built on the ground in Nepal. Thank you, Naim, John, Jeanne, Allison, Bidisa, Jen, SP, and Jaddon. I'm so proud of our work and so grateful to you for devoting your lives to our mission.

To the book team. Margaret, you are a wonderful friend and agent. Thank you for sticking by my side all these years and gently and patiently saying, "Whenever you're ready." Andrea, Amanda, and the rest of the team at Harper Horizon, thank you for believing in me and the power of this story. Shannon, you breathed so much life and humor and beauty into this book and made me seem like a way better writer. You gave this story its bones and heart and stepped in for me when there were things too hard to put into words. You are brilliant, and I'm so lucky our paths crossed to bring this book into the world.

To Jeremy, you are what dreams are made of, and I still have to pinch myself and you to make sure you're real. Thank you for being on this journey with me.

To my mom, dad, and sisters. Thank you for giving me a foundation of love and a truly happy childhood filled with bike rides, camping trips, stargazing, and adventure.

To my Canadian Power Regimbal family. How wonderful it's been to know, love, and be loved by you. Thank you for letting us move into the cabin during COVID times, and for the countless meals, laughs, and days of babysitting so I could focus on this project.

Roda, my forever best friend. Thank you for calling every single day, for reminding me to dream big and learn to love myself. Thank you for making me get out of bed, come to California, and move in with you, Tor, and the kids when I could barely stand. I love you and am forever in awe of the woman you are.

To Ruth and Hans Dekker. I have no idea where I'd be without you. Each and every step of the way, I thank my lucky stars for you both.

To Karen and Tom Mulvaney, thank you for your kindness, your heart, for investing and believing in me and our school all the way through.

To Leslie Shaw, thank you for always being a text and a call away, a sounding board and a shoulder to lean on. Jeremy Doppelt, you've been right along our side since the day we met. Thank you for working so hard and helping us finish off our dream school.

Eileen and Les Quick, I love you and your family with all my heart. Thank you, thank you for loving and believing in our family and for constantly going above and beyond for us.

To Jim and Beth Duff. Your love and compassion inspired so much of what stands of Kopila today and the legacy that will live on forever. Thank you.

To Kim and Finn Wentworth, meeting you changed the course of my life and the BlinkNow Foundation. You set me on the right track from the beginning and always reminded me to follow my heart.

Autumn, Nena, Luke, Jamie, Anjali, Cal, Kelly S., Chris, and Kelly D., Jeff D., Lexi, Anna, Kathleen, Patty, Franny, Julia, Meg, Caroline, Safira, Ben, Becky, John, and all the Kopila Fellows over the years. I wish I could have had six more chapters to talk about your shenanigans and our times together. Thank you for dedicating years of your lives to our work. You kept me sane and smiling and grounded and I love you all so much.

To every BlinkNow supporter who's ever been and ever will be. Everything we have ever done, built, and created; every child we have ever helped; and every brick, bunk bed, school uniform, warm pair of jammies, nutritious meal, and medical intervention has been because of your heart, generosity, and belief in our mission. Margaret Mead said, "Never doubt that a small group of thoughtful, committed citizens can change the world. Indeed, it's the only thing that ever has." And now I know that in my heart to be true.

ACKNOWLEDGMENTS

To our dream makers, monthly roots supporters, founding family, and Bodhi Tree Society, thank you for always being by our side through thick and thin, for investing in and sustaining our work and so much more.

Joke Aerts and Anuj Mittal

Roda Ahmed and Tor Hermansen

Dana Almatrook

Anna and Dean Backer

Mohamad and Nada Ballout

The Barer and Maisano Family

Linda and Bill Bartzak

The Bella Charitable Foundation

Anna Beuselinck and Gary Breen

Amund and Sunniva Bjorklund

Amiee Bloom

Debra and Andrew Breech

Laurie and Charlie Briggs

Dr. Melissa and Dr. David Brown

Susie and Robert Buckley

Steve Buffone

Joseph and Erika Campbell

Sara Carapezzi

Chip Carver and Anne DeLaney

Krishna Prasanth Chitta and Naga Venkata Sowmya

The Christmann Family

Leah and Chris Collier

Jeanne and Edwin Cooper

Libby DeLana

Alma DeMetropolis

Nancy and Bob Devine

Jeff DiLollo

Celeste Messina and Eric Dominioni

My uncle Ed Doyne and Aunt Lorraine

Acknowledgments

Larry Duff

Mark and Katie Duplass

Marie and David Dzanis

The Fairbairn Family

Mary Farrell

Ed and Amy Foye

The Furlong Family

Todd and Treacy Gaffney

Anita and Juan Galeana

Gretl Galgon

Rob and Laura Gawley

Elizabeth Gilbert

Matt Goldman and Renee
  Rolleri

Corinne Guerrette and Daniel
  Siehl

Prem and Juni Gurung

Ken Guthrie and Judy Reinsdorf

Margaret and Dr. Robert
  Hariri

Laurie Hay

Austin and Gabriela Hearst

Lauren Holden and Tom
  Kilbane

John Hollway and Jami McKeon

Beth Holly

Meredith Hostetter and
  Anthony Newman

Jolie Hughes

Kristen, John, and Kelsey
  Hyland

Brion and Sandy Johnson

Nico de Jong and family

Kristine Kadela

Marjorie and Michael Keith

Kathryn Kimber

Adrienne and Dillard Kirby

Rob Vogel and Carrie Kitze

Monique Kovaks and Ari
  Nathan

Tirza Kramer and Ari Skromne

Nicholas Kristof

Acknowledgments

Heidi Krump

Steven and Chani Laufer

Salli LeVan and Michael Steck

Brian Lindstrom and Cheryl
Strayed

Chris and Jim MacDonald

Lowell McAdam

Sean McLaughlin

Rachel Miner

Amy and Vincent Molinaro

Claudia Mott

Christopher Nordloh and Kate
Ortner

Donn and Vicky Norton

Regina Pauly

Ronald Penl

Michael and Jane Pharr

Random Acts

Dave and Megan Sager

Nancy and Nelson Schaenen

Stephen and Sheila Schlageter

Joel Seaman

Michael and Kathleen Seergy

Dr. Sanjib and Mrs. Soni
Shrestha

Bill and Cindy Simon

J. Peter and Janet Simon

Iris and Michael Smith

Margaret Smith

Tara Smith and Brian Swibel

Barbara and Lance Sullivan

Jagdish Upadhyay

Dieuwke Van Putten

Jeffrey Walker

Christopher and Lorraine
Wilson

Doon and Nancy Wintz

The Aviv Foundation

Bucketlist Bombshells

Community Foundation of
Tampa Bay

Compassionate Service Society

ACKNOWLEDGMENTS

CVC Advisors

Emily C. Specchio Foundation

February Foundation

The Fine and Greenwald
    Foundation

Galesi Family Foundation

Grant Me the Wisdom
    Foundation

Kathryn B. McQuade
    Foundation

Mara W Breech Foundation

MCJ Amelior Foundation

The Peck School

She's the First

Together Women Rise

The Wilson Sheehan Foundation

About BlinkNow

Our story starts on a dry riverbed in the foothills of the Himalayas where a young girl needed help to attend school. That one simple act, enrolling a girl in school, grew into hope for a community of people who deserved the opportunity for improved livelihoods. Soon, others followed, and our acts of service blossomed into the BlinkNow Foundation, a nonprofit serving a growing, ever-inspiring community in Surkhet, Nepal. Over the last fourteen years, we've designed programs to realize our mission through education, family support, and a holistic approach to community development.

BlinkNow has received its fair share of great praise and occasional criticisms. We believe both are vital to our success. Some of the feedback has been incredibly constructive and has made our organization better; some of it has been unfounded and harmful to our mission. We continually assess our role in the perpetuation of the white savior industrial complex and remain committed to empowering the Nepali community we serve. We show this commitment with our large team of Nepali staff and leadership at every level of the organization and representation on our Nepal-based board.

For more information on our team, history, strategic plan, and financials, visit BlinkNow.org.

OUR PROGRAMS

Since 2007, BlinkNow's unique model ensures that no child's needs fall through the cracks. Our children have gone on to become engineers, school principals, medical workers, and so much more. They are shaping the future of Nepal. All our work is infused with our core organizational values of **gender equality, economic empowerment, and environmental sustainability.**

The **Kopila Valley School** is educating a generation of thoughtful, inspired change-makers by nurturing the whole child—the head, the heart, and the hand. We know that education gives kids the power to shape their futures. BlinkNow's Kopila Valley School provides free, high-quality education to over five hundred students. Starting at early childhood, students are equipped with the skills, knowledge, confidence, and social aptitude to bloom into successful, economically independent adults.

As the Kopila Valley School grew and needed a new campus, we realized it was a unique chance to put our values into physical form. We assembled a passionate team of innovative thinkers to design and build a school that modeled our commitment to the environment. From solar cooking systems to rainwater harvesting and water recycling to rammed earth walls that promote natural heating and cooling, every aspect of the campus demonstrates our commitment to advancing sustainable practices. We have built the greenest school in Nepal and one of the greenest in the world.

Our curriculum is enhanced by seasoned educational experts deeply committed to providing a well-rounded learning experience. Not only do we ensure aptitude in core subjects such as English and math, but we incorporate lessons in environmental science, outdoor learning, and sustainability.

Our **Health and Wellness Program** is integrated throughout our work. After opening our school, we realized that kids wouldn't regularly attend school until they were healthy and properly nourished. Many students relied on energy from a single daily meal! We started a healthy school food program providing high-quality produce and traditional meals to students daily. We also launched a clinic to promote healthcare: diagnosing symptoms, dressing minor injuries, and performing regular deworming camps, physicals, and specialist referrals. Our team of social workers manages relationships with our students' guardians, providing counsel in times of crisis or conflict. Through constant case management and emotional care, our students have the support system they need to build healthy lives.

Our **Kopila Valley Women's Center** provides job training and education in a supportive environment for women in our community. We empower women through skills-based training, entrepreneurship, counseling services, and workshops that cover a wide range of topics including women's rights, gender equality, family planning, and mental health. We are empowering women with the tools, skills, and knowledge to overcome social inequality and gain economic independence.

Our **Futures Center** guides our students through important academic and professional decisions during their formative years. After tenth grade, students narrow their career paths by enrolling in upper secondary programs or vocational training. Naturally, this time in life sparks curiosity, introspection, and exploration for our students. At the Futures Center, our academic counseling team prepares and supports students through these decisions, in many instances as their singular mentor in life. Using a combination of 1:1 counseling sessions, personal development workshops, strength and character examinations, career guest speakers, and mentor matching, we strive to broaden each student's awareness of possibilities, both nationally and internationally, as they plan their future. Due to the demographics of our students, attending university is an unlikely luxury without outside financial support. Through our Higher Education Fund, some of our students are awarded full-ride scholarships to attend the university of their choosing. All of these program elements together realize our dream to further the opportunities of Nepali children.

Our **Sustainability** programing is committed to creating a beautiful and enduring environment in which to live and a more sustainable future for our children. We have adapted to a place-based learning curriculum and work collaboratively across all of our program areas to be the best, most environmentally and ecologically sustainable organization we can be. We host an environmental ambassadors program and we partner with the local community, farmers, and the government to promote environmentally sustainable practices.

Our **Kopila Valley Children's Home** provides a loving family home to over fifty children. A dedicated team of caregivers, aunties, and uncles manages daily life at the home. Our young adults transition to independent living as they prepare for their bright futures and careers.

Our Big Sisters' Home provides a safe environment for a small group of female students who are at elevated risk for dropping out of school due to challenges including child marriage, child labor, and physical and emotional abuse. We provide a community of support, friendship, and healing that allows the girls to improve their studies and prepare for reintegration into their community and biological families.

ABOUT BLINKNOW

OUR MISSION

Our mission is to change the world by empowering Nepal's children. We do this by providing quality education and a loving, caring home for orphaned and at-risk children. We also support our local community to reduce poverty, empower women, and improve health, while encouraging sustainability and social justice.

OUR VISION

A world where every child is safe, educated, and loved.

BlinkNow Timeline

A BRIEF HISTORY

2007

Maggie Doyne and Tope Malla form a Kopila Valley board of directors and establish a Nepal-based NGO.

By June, the community breaks ground on the Kopila Valley Children's Home.

By August, BlinkNow is incorporated as a US nonprofit with a US board of directors.

By the end of the year, funding is established for the first floor of the home.

2008

Kopila Valley Children's Home takes its first child into care.

By July, there is a second floor on the home and three additional rooms.

A medically fragile child (Juntara) is taken for care in the UK.

2009

Maggie wins Cosmo Girls of the Year and uses the funding to expand the home. The number of children expands to thirty.

Maggie wins the Do Something Award, establishing $100,000 for building a new school.

2010

Kopila Valley School opens its doors.

Nick Kristof's article "D.I.Y. Foreign Aid Revolution" features Maggie and BlinkNow on the cover of the *New York Times* Sunday magazine.

2011

The Kopila Valley Clinic is established.

The Kopila Valley Fellows Program is established and brings long-term international volunteers to serve at Kopila.

2012

BlinkNow gains its first paid staff person, Maggie.

Manisha dies by suicide (November).

Kopila Valley School acquires its first school bus (December 25).

2013

Kopila Valley Women's Empowerment Center is established.

BlinkNow office is opened in Morristown, New Jersey. Ruth is hired in April, followed by Jeanne (the first paid staff after Maggie).

A beautiful plot of land is purchased to create a permanent home for Kopila Valley School.

A deep well is dug on the new land.

Farming begins on the land.

2014

Construction begins on the new green campus with a clear focus on sustainability.

A social worker helps to establish a mental health program at Kopila.

Maggie's op-ed piece about suicide appears in the *New York Times* (March).

Ravi comes to Kopila severely malnourished (July).

Surkhet is hit by a catastrophic flood and the team acts as first responders in the community (August).

BlinkNow Futures Program is established to successfully transition our children in the home and school into their next phase of life.

Ravi comes for medical treatment to the US (December).

2015

A 7.8 magnitude earthquake devastates Nepal (April).

BlinkNow is registered as an INGO.

BlinkNow graduates its first class of tenth graders (June) and establishes a scholarship program for graduates to continue their education in their chosen fields.

Maggie receives the CNN Hero of the Year Award (December).

Ravi passes away in a terrible accident (December 30).

2016

The Floortje Dessing show airs in the Netherlands and our base of support there skyrockets.

A Kopila graduate is admitted to boarding school in the Netherlands.

Kopila Valley School expands to offer a new "Plus Two" management program.

2017

Our first Kopila graduates head to university, including one to the US on a full scholarship.

The doors of a Big Sister's Home for at-risk girls open.

(Maggie and Jeremy are married.)

BlinkNow celebrates its tenth anniversary with its first ever gala.

Women's center graduates form their own cooperative.

2018

BlinkNow completes construction of classrooms on its new Green Campus and begins to transition students from the Bamboo School location.

(Ruby Sunshine is born.)

2019

Kopila Valley School celebrates the grand opening of its Green Campus.

The Early Childhood Village is completed and Kopila expands to provide high quality care for infants and toddlers.

BlinkNow completes a ten-year strategic plan.

2020

The BlinkNow team becomes first responders in a migrant crisis and provides humanitarian aid to those affected by the COVID pandemic.

Our first endowment fund is established.

Kopila Valley School and programs transition to remote learning and service provision.

About the Authors

MAGGIE DOYNE IS cofounder of the BlinkNow Foundation and Kopila Valley Children's Home and School in Surkhet, Nepal. At age nineteen, she used her life savings to build a home for orphaned children in war-torn Nepal. In 2010, she and her team opened a school for five hundred of the region's most impoverished children. Throughout the past decade, BlinkNow and Kopila have worked to deepen and grow the organization through grassroots community development efforts.

Her work has been championed by Pulitzer Prize–winning columnist Nicholas Kristof and the Dalai Lama, among others. The story of BlinkNow's beginnings has been featured on the *Huffington Post*, VH1, MTV, and DoSomething.org. Maggie was named *Glamour* magazine's Woman of the Year and was used as an example for her groundbreaking work at the Forbes 400 Summit on Philanthropy, where she was named one of the thirty most influential people under thirty. In 2015, she was named CNN Hero of the Year.

Maggie's story carries a message of hope, love, and the possibility of how the smallest individual acts can spark huge world change. She believes that poverty, hunger, and violence will be alleviated when children are provided with their most basic needs and human rights—a loving, happy childhood, nutrition, and a quality education. She believes that this can be achieved during her lifetime.

———

SHANNON LEE MILLER is a bestselling developmental editor and writer living in East Nashville, Tennessee, with her husband and three wild kiddos. When she's not deep in a book, she (mostly) enjoys running marathons, growing vegetables, and learning to be a better ally to underrepresented communities.

There is no time to waste. If you are educated and free, empowered and safe, you have to use your strength, your power, and your gifts to help the rest of our human family.

—Maggie Doyne